To the memory of Roy Landau
Friend, philosopher, architect and guide
Michael Pearson

The Power of
Process:
The Architecture of
Michael Pearson

Chris Rogers

**black dog
publishing**
london uk

Contents

1 | introduction

Change. It is often said to be the only constant in life; in architecture, it is the lynchpin around which debate and advance occur, as the present separates from the past. For the past five decades, change has had a very special meaning for Michael Pearson.

He has moved from architectural student to second youngest president of the Architectural Association (AA) and from 28 year old partner in the firm headed by his father and founded by his grandfather to principal of that family practice working on multi-million pound schemes in Britain and abroad. He has contended with being a practising architect through the oil crisis of the 1970s, the political turmoil in Africa and the Middle East during the same period and recessions since. He has lived in Britain, France and the United States, been married three times, had major heart surgery and been forced to relocate his home and business and sell family assets to survive.

Throughout, change has also played a central role in his architecture. Believing that a building's "occupant is an unpredictable person" and that a building must therefore adapt freely to differing demands throughout its life to make it truly useful and economic, Pearson has striven to imbue all of his designs from the outset — regardless of typology, scale or budget — with the ability to accept change, often looking beyond initial function and occupier.[1] In doing so, he has recognised and adopted an effective working definition of change:

> Flexibility is something that's bendable; adaptability is something that's changeable, particularly internally; if you're talking about internal flexibility it really has to be adaptability. And then you can have extendibility....[2]

The work arising from this element of Pearson's philosophy ranges from a subtle, contextual addition to a period house in an English village through a groundbreaking, competition-winning scheme for a column-free, adaptable office to his masterwork, Burne House telecommunications centre, a building which pioneered fully interchangeable cladding, was far ahead of noted 'High-Tech' architects in this field and which Pearson describes as "The most important thing I've done."[3] Projects around the world followed, maintaining this element and adding others.

However, acceptance of and allowance for change are not only fundamental qualities of Pearson's buildings, they are central to the very method he employs to create them.

First, his initial conceptual response to the brief is committed to paper: "Drawings are a way of defining problems; without drawings you can't see what the problems are."[4]

Such problems are honestly welcomed by Pearson as a means of making progress against the original brief, and in this he draws a fascinating parallel with the investigative methodology he learned in school science classes, whereby

> posing a hypothesis certainly made you focus [...] to see whether you could prove it. The hypothesis created problems, and it is a problem-solving process to get to an acceptable result within the criteria [when designing a building].[5]

By contrast, Pearson robustly dismisses contemporary coyness over the word "problem":

> I keep going round talking about problems on these jobs, and [client] project managers that must have been to some management course [say] 'No no we don't have any problems at all, we have challenges'.[6]

The revised concept is then subjected to challenge by, and discussion with, the client and end users before being modified again or discarded. This iterative approach continues until a mutually agreed solution emerges, one which is invariably much closer to

Michael Pearson.

clients' and users' needs than any arising from other, more autocratic, modes of engagement. It is only possible following the realisation that "Architecture is a compromise."[7] Thoughtful and effective, this method has inspired the present work's title.

Yet change and process are only part of the Pearson story. In asking "What we're doing, why we're doing it and how did we get there", one must look for more clues.[8] Very few architects come to their subject entirely without influence or able to bury that influence so deeply that many are unaware of it. John Soane was one, Edwin Lutyens arguably another. Both had a singular persistence of vision that seemed independent of others and outside the norm.

For most architects, though, their concept of their craft involves absorption of the work of those others that Soane and Lutyens appeared to eschew, taking—however subconsciously—elements that appeal, ideas that intrigue and shapes that delight and mixing these with the unique talent that each in their own right possesses. The result is their personal practice of the art of architecture, with some aspects prominent and others suppressed.

For Pearson, this absorption has had an even deeper meaning as the third generation of his family to head the architectural practice founded by his paternal grandfather, Charles Bulman Pearson, in Lancaster in 1904. Charles B Pearson designed private houses, commercial premises, halls, war memorials and a school before partnering with his son, Charles Edward Pearson, Michael's father. Separately and together they worked on projects private and public, large and small, achieving particular success with competition entries for civic schemes such as town halls, schools and hospitals. Many were built and all laid the foundations for the firm's direction after the Second World War.

Charles B (as he became known in the pragmatic style of address favoured by the family) showed a keen sense of connection to his home county but travelled to the United States as early as the 1920s researching new developments, and showed aptitude for working with clients and determining their needs. Charles E led teams of architects on large projects, had a talent for adaptable internal planning and was concerned with the locale for which he designed. Both were superb draughtsmen of elevations, perspectives and measured drawings.

Thus for Charles Michael Pearson — "Charles" disappeared from use at an early age — the inheritance of others was of a rare depth, recalling perhaps only the Gilbert Scott dynasty.[9] He was to follow in his grandfather's and father's footsteps in almost every way and demonstrate many of the same abilities, yet develop a philosophy clearly his own which would include building a close relationship with the client or end user, sensitive consideration of a site and an unusually informed view of service provision.

For Pearson a clear set of architectural principles, a rewarding working method and a rich and very personal heritage has resulted in a wide range of schemes which will be explored in the following pages.

Pearson's teaching career at, and subsequent presidency of the AA, and his pivotal role in the fight for its independence, his friendship with major British figures of the period including Cedric Price, Jim Stirling and Roy Landau and enthusiastic contact with international architects such as Louis Kahn and Ezra Ehrenkrantz and designer Jean Prouvé and his strong theoretical and conceptual background round out this fascinating practitioner who moved in a critical phase of post-war British architecture.

Michael Pearson continues to practise today. After 50 years his enthusiasm for architecture, the purity of his thinking and the values underlying both are undiminished and remain as deeply embedded in his work as they have always done, as *The Power of Process* seeks to show.

1   MP, quoted in "The Architect V The Housewife, Ideal Home", c. 1970.
2   MP, in conversation with the author, 1 March 2008, quoting — from memory — an article written by another.
3   MP, in conversation with the author, 22 January 2008.
4   MP, in conversation with the author, 1 March 2008.
5   MP, in conversation with the author, 29 February 2008.
6   MP, in conversation with the author, 29 February 2008. The careful reader will note that the author, suitably warned, avoids this use of the word "challenge" in the present work.
7   MP, in conversation with the author, 12 August 2007.
8   MP, in conversation with the author, 7 August 2007.
9   George Gilbert Scott, 1811–1878, his grandsons Giles Gilbert Scott, 1880–1960, and Adrian Gilbert Scott, 1882–1963, and Giles's son Richard Gilbert Scott, born 1923.

2 | Inheritance

Charles B Pearson's elevations for his competition entry design for the new London County Council's home; grand but, even at 55 bays' width, not overbearing.

I was very pleased to have your letter of the 8th inst and to find that the little efforts I have made during the last seven or eight years on behalf of Charles have gratified you and Mrs Pearson: Charles' success is almost entirely due to his own perseverance and aptitude & I think that if he continues to make progress he should in time become a thoroughly competent draughtsman and architectural assistant.[1]

When noted Lancaster architect E Howard Dawson wrote this cautious but warm assessment of the 20 year old Charles Bulman Pearson in 1896, he clearly appreciated the nascent talents of a young man who had come from a farming family but whose keenness to become an architect had resulted in him working in Dawson's office as an articled pupil.

Employed thereafter as Lancaster Borough Surveyor's assistant and, when that proved insufficiently stimulating, at various architects' practices in Carlisle, Hull and London, Pearson simultaneously secured the first of many local and national prizes for his architectural drawing, an early indication of a family trait. In succeeding years he undertook training at Lancaster's Storey Institute and, from 1901, the Royal Academy.

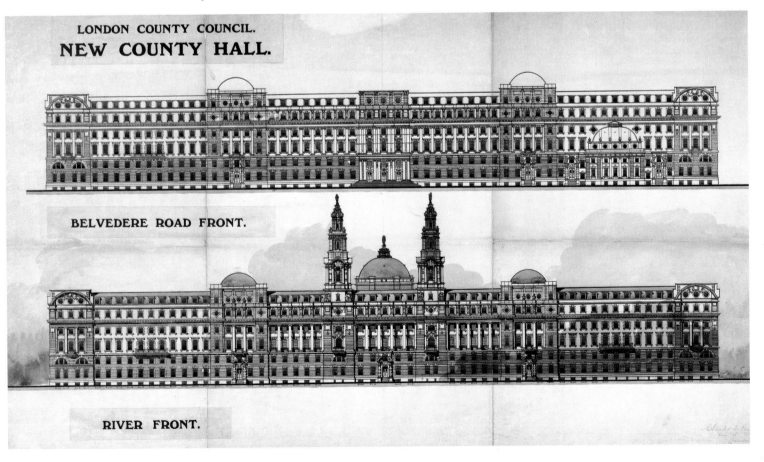

LONDON COUNTY COUNCIL.
NEW COUNTY HALL.

BELVEDERE ROAD FRONT.

RIVER FRONT.

INVERLUNE + ALDCLIFF
Fer E. B. DAWSON ESQRE
CHARLES B. PEARSON
ARCHITECT LANCASTER

Above
The south front of Inverlune,
Pearson's house for EB Dawson
of 1910, with its jaunty tower.

Opposite top
An example of Pearson's
measured drawing skill is this
recording of the choir stalls from
the priory church, Lancaster,
which was published nationally.

Opposite bottom
Charles B Pearson's sketch of
a proposed extension of the
west end of St Mary's priory and
parish church, Lancaster.

After marriage and initial settlement in Hull, Pearson returned to Lancaster where, in 1904, he set up his own practice and, later, home in the city's elegant Georgian Dalton Square, where a new town hall would soon take shape to neo-Classical designs by EW Mountfield and with interiors by Waring and Gillow, firms founded in Liverpool and Lancaster respectively.

In these stimulating surroundings, Pearson worked initially on new village halls. He did not lack ambition, however, and in 1907, a year after becoming a Tite Medallist, he entered the London County Council's competition for its new County Hall with an imposing yet delicately detailed design that combined awareness of the past with, even at this early stage, a sure sense of his own style. The beautiful elevations he prepared for the assessors depict a confident principal facade of Classical, Beaux-Arts derivation, its immense extent softened by being frequently broken forward and by rustication, carefully deployed pilasters and circular windows. This last would become a favourite motif. Two towers, thin and ecclesiastical, flank a central dome to centre the piece. Although unplaced, the entry signalled a flair for competitions which would soon yield rewards.

Pearson's first major built work, a large country house commissioned by Edward B Dawson, Lancaster county magistrate and father of his former master, confirmed that he was equally comfortable in the more homely Arts and Crafts vein. The house, called Inverlune after Lancaster's river Lune, is situated in the grounds of the Dawson family seat, Aldcliffe Hall, and was built for Dawson's youngest child and her husband. In designing it in 1910 it is likely that Pearson was drawing on at least two local works by the great CFA Voysey: Broad Leys, 1898, and Moor Crag, 1899, both at Windermere. Pearson used Voysey trademarks such as deep bay windows breaking into the roofline, small dormer windows and prominent, distinctive chimneys, although these are a feature of vernacular Lake District architecture and so show both artists' partiality to regional tradition. Here again, though, Pearson created an original work by the use of tile banding on his chimney tops, and a delightful half-timbered tower with open top floor on the south facade took advantage of the magnificent unobstructed views that remain available to Inverlune's occupants today.

A curious but telling offshoot of this job was Pearson's 1914 competition design for reinforced concrete cottages. A mature material but still relatively rare, Dawson senior had in fact been building with it since 1878 and it must be assumed that Pearson was aware of this. This enthusiasm of Pearson for modern practices was to reappear, and would also mark out his son.

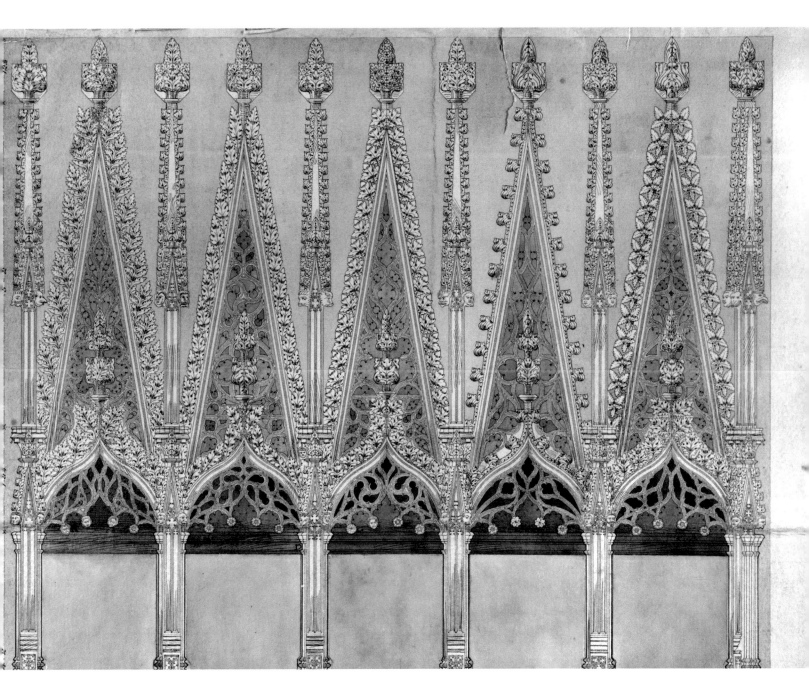

Proposed Cathedral for Lancaster
Suggested Extension of St Mary's

"Moorgarth". Lancaster · for Mrs. T. Cook.

Charles E. Pearson. F.R.I.B.A.
Architect
Dalton Square Lancaster.

Pearson's war service as a lieutenant in the Royal Garrison Artillery gave rise, unsurprisingly, to sketched designs for war memorials in a simple Classical language of columns, obelisks and pediments but also, in 1918, to an audacious proposal for an entire new cathedral for Manchester, to serve as memorial, civic symbol and even, by the effort of its construction, contributor to the economy. On the empty Piccadilly Gardens site, the new building would be "built in the most English of Ecclesiastical styles, Gothic at its zenith" to harmonise with Alfred Waterhouse's grandiose town hall, 1877, and Basil Champneys' John Rylands Library, 1899.[2]

Pearson's love of Gothic and his home town also caused him to suggest remodelling Lancaster's priory and parish church, which he considered "of poor detail and erected when Gothic architecture was at a very low ebb", to secure cathedral city status and adapting the adjacent castle as a residence for the Duke of Lancaster.[3]

Opposite

Moorgarth, one of a number
of private house commissions
executed by Charles B, was
illustrated beautifully by Charles
in this perspective which was
shown at the Royal Academy.
Designed in 1931 and sited just
north of Williamson Park in
Lancaster, Moorgarth employs
Charles B's familiar circular
windows and banded chimneys
but is otherwise more restrained
in decoration and is almost
entirely symmetrical in plan
and in elevation, reflecting a
more Modern approach for
the practice.

Bottom

The first major competition
success for the newly-partnered
father and son, Ramsey Grammar
School is an elegant neo-Classical
arrangement; the swan-neck
pediment from Moorgarth
reappears. This perspective by
Charles E was exhibited at the
Royal Academy.

In 1920, Pearson achieved second place in a
competition for Southport Secondary School with an
attractive, two-storey, quietly Classical design whose
exterior displayed Pearson's beloved circular windows
and tile-banded chimneys but whose clarity of plan
reveals another skill which would come to distinguish
the Pearsons.

Pearson now began to be employed by fellow
architects as a competition expert and in other capacities,
for example contributing to and illustrating Campbell
Jones, Son & Smithers' scheme for the Lloyds Bank portion
of the Guardian Assurance Company building on a
prestigious site facing London Bridge in the City of London.[4]

The following year's award of the Godwin Bursary
enabled Pearson to travel to the United States to
study new thinking in hotel design, whilst at home
work included more private houses, extending
the vocabulary used at Inverlune, and a broader
range of building types including a new cinema in
Carnforth, six miles north of Lancaster, with giant
order Ionic pilasters and a warehouse in Lancaster
with a contextual main facade but whose extensively
glazed side elevations echoed Peter Behrens' AEG
turbine factory, Berlin, of 1909.

This prolific output of residential, commercial and
civic schemes, some of which he illustrated in works

The jazz age at Morecambe;
the Pearsons' designs for a
new pavilion on the pier.

exhibited at the Royal Academy, continued until the
1926 General Strike forced him to London. Here he was
joined by his son, Charles Edward Pearson, who had
been born in 1907 and educated at Lancaster Royal
Grammar School before working for Lancashire County
Council as the first step in his own architectural career.

Initially articled to his father, Charles E formally
joined Charles B in partnership in 1931 whereafter
Charles B Pearson & Son entered many competitions
with designs underpinned by intelligence, utility
and efficiency. Indeed that same year the pair won
first prize for Ramsey Grammar School on the Isle of
Man, melding Charles B's finely detailed neo-Classical
exteriors with Charles E's own emerging facility for
internal planning. Ramsey can be identified as the
beginning of the Pearson legacies of civic projects and
competition success, and the young Charles E also
produced an exquisite perspective rendering of the
scheme, demonstrating another pleasing inheritance.

Probably under Charles E's lead and almost
certainly reflecting Oliver Hill's landmark Midland
Hotel along the shore completed in 1933, their
rebuilding of Morecambe's Central Pier in 1934 saw
the New Dance Pavilion erected, with strip windows,
exuberant light fixtures atop streamlined pylons
bordering the stage and dramatic ribbed barrel-
vaulted ceiling.

This was not a tipping point toward Modernism,
though, a neo-Classical sensibility remaining in the
Pearsons' third-placed entry for a new Public Hall for
Harpenden, Hertfordshire two years later. However,
the winning design adopted a fresher aesthetic that
looked to emergent continental themes and, whilst
its author was to return to the Pearson story in a most
unexpected manner nearly 40 years later, as covered
in chapter six, the lesson learned showed in one of
two winning entries just before the Second World War
which together summarised the history and set out
the future direction of the Pearson practice.

Above
Early sketch of the building with walls constructed from angle iron and hardboard, an early example of lightweight construction.

Opposite
Interior views showing roof lights between the arches.

The Pearsons' 1936 Llandudno hospital showed superior ability in planning for the complex, inter-related functions of a hospital. Specialist departments were situated to one side of the entrance hall, staff and support accommodation to the other. Beds were grouped and each ward was provided with its own, localised kitchen and bathroom.

Considerations of flexibility and future change were paramount. Expansion was planned from the outset, doubling the number of beds, and layout and servicing allowed for this with a second wing to house the additional patients and the boiler room, kitchen and laundry sized to cope with that expansion when it occurred.

Llandudno was built, completing in 1939. A letter written by the chairman of its finance committee to both Pearsons reflects the appreciation he had for these Lancastrian architects and by implication the importance which they attached to client relations:

Dear Messrs Pearson (Senior & Junior)

It is with mixed feelings that I write you today, sending you the final commission cheque in relation to the completion of the New Hospital Contract.

I am very glad of course that this very important work has been so satisfactorily carried out under your supervision, and that we all have great pride in the completed job.

I have several times assured you of our absolute faith and trust in your firm's efficiency and integrity, and now again confirm it.

But I am sad that our association has come to an end, and that we shall not see so much of you both. The association over this Hospital has been one of my life's keenest satisfactions, and I shall always remember you and your families with pleasure.

I wish Mr. & Mrs. C.B. many more years of good health and pleasure in seeing Mr. & Mrs. C.E. move forward from success to success. Many many thanks for your very great help at all times during the contract.

Kindest regards — always.

Yours sincerely,
(R.C. Baxter)

Hon. Sec.[5]

The project also began the practice's particular association with the hospital as a building type.

The second win, in 1937, was for Scunthorpe Civic Centre. Here, a subtly asymmetric composition of brick with stone detailing was assembled from a central block, itself asymmetrical, and two unmatched wings projecting forward, each with their own entrances.

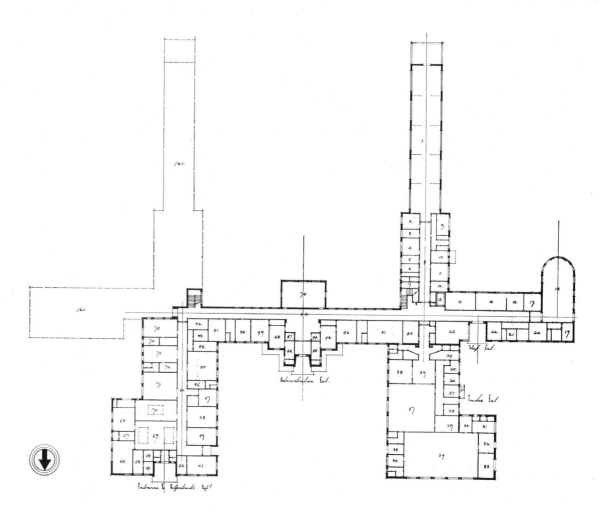

Above
Ground floor plan of Llandudno hospital with expansion provision depicted to the southeast.

Opposite
The entrance with patterned brickwork and fired clay pilasters. Glazed operating theatre is on first floor above.

The whole was strongly reminiscent of contemporary British town halls in layout (Walthamstow, London by Philip Hepworth, competition 1932, begun 1937), materials (Hornsey, London by Reginald Uren, Slater and Moberley, 1935–1937) and detail (Norwich, by CH James and S Rowland Pierce, finished 1938 but published in 1932).

It is unlikely that Charles B or Charles E were ignorant of all of these buildings, especially as, remembering Harpenden, they were designs influenced by Dutchman Willem Dudok and Swede Ragnar Östberg. Yet none of this takes away from the very individual and very elegant building which the Pearsons produced, an elegance brought out once more in Charles E's seductive perspectives. That it again accorded closely with the client's wishes is evidenced by the fact that separate police buildings, originally intended to be carried out by the county architect with the competition winner only as consultant, were handed to Charles B Pearson & Son to design in their entirety. Thus did the individual attitudes of two architects and their shared talents—of design and drawing, of collaboration and

interaction, of questioning and investigation—create an exceptional foundation for the decades to come.

The outbreak of war halted construction of the Scunthorpe scheme, but only temporarily. When architecture became possible again, its design would be dramatically revisited in a new style for a new era, an era in which the third generation of Pearson would arrive to work alongside his father in turn.

1   Edward Howard Dawson, letter to Thomas Pearson, 9 December 1896.
2   Charles B Pearson, Suggestion for a war memorial in Manchester, brochure, 1918.
3   Charles B Pearson, A vision of the future Lancaster Priory & Parish Church as a Cathedral, handwritten notes, undated.
4   Although at this time Campbell Jones, Son & Smithers' involvement in the scheme had not been confirmed due to debate by the bank's directors, Pearson received payment of £52.10 for his work at the express desire of W Campbell Jones himself.
5   Letter, RC Baxter to Messrs. CB Pearson & Son, 18 May 1940.

N E W · C I V I C · C E N T R E · S

Top
Hornsey Town Hall.

Bottom
Walthamstow Civic Centre;
two contemporary town hall
references.

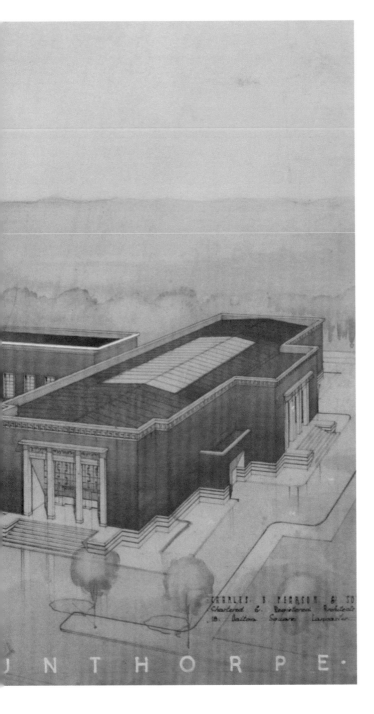

3|Life

Complementing the key dates listed elsewhere, the vignettes below—mostly in Pearson's own words—aim to highlight periods in his life which developed his attitude to architecture and illuminate later chapters.

Landscape

> Bolton-le-Sands was a little tiny village with an old church and the turnpike road going north went through there and then the A6 [...] And, you know, having a pretty reasonable hill immediately outside the back garden and then endless trees and land to go roaming in... I think that was the very significant thing.[1]

Inheritance

> [I was] aware of father working every night at his drawing board on a reproduction oak table with huge girth turned legs and quarter leaf extensions at each end, which amazed me.[2] I think that's where it started [After visiting] Blackpool and St Annes [I] planned an hotel in rather crude terms [...] I would have been seven.[3]

Components

> [We] were really energetic constructors of all sorts of things; we had to make our own, there was nothing around [...] In the Scouts we went off at a camp and we were given three poles and a bit of rope and told to get across that stream without getting our feet wet, so you have to understand the mechanics of an A-frame [...] I always had an early interest in mechanics.[4]

Method

Pearson studied physics, chemistry and mathematics at A-level. He found it "creates a way of thinking about things [which] I'm sure I've benefited from".[5]

Drawing

Manchester's architecture course fell under Professor RA Cordingley, an eminent historian and Rome scholar. Developing a talent he had shown at school, Pearson therefore learnt how to draw,

> and that is not taught, as far as I can tell, by anybody these days [We] had to do compositions of different porticos—Ionic and Corinthian [...]—on paper stretched on the drawing board and apply watercolour washes, [...] up to 50 washes on the sky to get it right, [but] it was wonderful for me, because [...] I can do any projection or perspective, I can do axonometric and [...] skiagraphy, projected shadows on the fronts of buildings and around curved elements.[6]

Modernism

> Bill [Cowburn] and I used to set off on the midnight train together, arrive at Euston at four o'clock, go to the Lyons Corner House in the Strand which was the only one open all night, and get up to Highgate and be looking at the flats at Highgate when everybody was getting up, they thought we were spies, six o'clock we were there with our cameras and binoculars.[7] And then we got the next overnight train back.[8]

Contacts

Aged 21 Pearson began, with Cowburn and Tony Travis, a planning student, *244*, a magazine titled after the school of architecture's former address. Pearson summarised their motivation later: "We just wanted our say."[9]

Pearson secured articles from some of the world's most prominent designers for its seven editions. Issue one alone featured architect Walter Gropius and Edgar J Kaufmann, Jnr, for whose father Frank Lloyd Wright had designed the great house Fallingwater and who was himself a director of the Museum of Modern Art in New York, whilst for British sculptor Eduardo Paolozzi this was "the first time that a magazine has mixed my applied design work & 'fine art'".[10]

Pearson invited similar figures to lecture to the student body, including sculptor Reg Butler and Hugh Casson, who had recently been director of architecture for the Festival of Britain and whose arrival at the university on the back of Pearson's Lambretta, having accepted Pearson's offer to "meet you at the station" in the expectation of a somewhat more conventional means of conveyance, evidently did not affect his willingness to speak.[11]

In such startlingly informal, clubbable times, Pearson particularly appreciated the help of architect James Stirling for whom he worked at Lyons, Israel & Ellis during a vacation and who remained a "great support and a great friend. He set up these meetings with the rich and famous in the States when I went, because he was teaching at Harvard".[12]

Practice
For Pearson, humility in architecture was vital from the beginning: "One likes to be harsh about one's own work to see whether it stands up to criticism".[13]

Teaching I
In 1962, Pearson approached AA principal William Allen regarding a post as unit master. After Allen asked him to join the jury assessing the final thesis of John Outram, a student of James Gowan, Pearson got the job, later including "The only working drawings programme at that time and probably the last".[14] Pearson's didactics mirrored his embryonic practice, since

> the whole principle of our teaching [was] a heuristic experience for the students through design projects, that they would come along and they would put forward what they were attempting to do, their

objectives, [...] very clearly, and then at juries we tested whether their solution stood up to their original criteria.[15]

Pearson feels this was also a valuable way of "eradicating architectural arrogance".[16] Satisfyingly, it emulated the fundamental basis of science he learned at school—posit a theory, design an experiment to test it, then analyse the results to see if these validate the theory.

Pearson's year master at this time and for three years overall at the AA was architect Roy Landau. Born in 1927, Landau had worked for Paul Rudolph in the United States and married intellectual rigour and curiosity—about philosophy, complexity, computing—to practicality. He brought new modes of learning, notably systems theory (working together to produce an outcome) and cybernetics (how action is continually modified by feedback), to the AA which fitted perfectly with Pearson's own thoughts. In a period when theories—social, intellectual, scientific—were everything yet any connection to reality might sometimes have appeared tenuous, Landau grounded certain of these and also ensured, with Pearson, that students were never hobbled by linear thinking:

> We were trying to get students to think inductively rather than deductively [as, with the latter,] you've never finished, you've never done enough analysis; the time has got to come where you've got to put pencil to paper and see what it makes for you [...] Rather than deducing from the last one, which everybody does, can you approach it from a sideways position?[17]

Pearson established a great friendship with Landau, later developing with him the concept underpinning Burne House and its cladding.

Time

Pearson and Landau felt "devising 'once-and-for-all' physical forms which would meet the expected needs of the user [by] a simple matter of proficient initial design"[18] was unrealistic for an architect, emerging evidence envisaging increasing unpredictability "over a period of time which may or (more likely) may not be determinable".[19] They accordingly asked "what forms of conceptualisation can he adopt?".[20]

Two models were proposed for a new, time-based architecture. The first, true to their AA teaching, thought laterally but thoroughly:

> The stimulus-response model would conceptualise a building as a closed system with as wide a range of user possibilities as the initial conception of the building was able to foresee and to afford. Thus, for a whole range of after-completion demands by the user, there would exist a latent capacity in the building for response.[21]

Though still restricted by those initial considerations, they believed "possibilities are inherently richer" with this approach, a richness which was to have its realisation in Burne House.[22]

However, even this was not intended to be the limit of the two architects' vision. More radical, the second, "evolutionary", model "does not have an ultimate capacity or a final state built into it. It is user-regulated, open-ended and must possess the capability for the intake of new resources as new needs occur".[23]

Both represented "a move from a static idea of 'state' towards a dynamic idea of 'process'", and thus had an obvious attraction for Pearson.[24]

Research I

Emulating his grandfather Pearson travelled to the United States in 1962 for research, investigating American blockwork techniques for his sponsor,

the Cement and Concrete Association. This would yield dividends for two of his buildings, but Pearson also seized the opportunity, facilitated by Stirling, to meet the great Louis Kahn, whose very personal architecture Pearson had admired for some time.

> I met Kahn at his office, spent a whole Saturday morning with him, went to have a look at his physics laboratory at University of Pennsylvania, then went to a concrete block school at East Liverpool where he was using preformed metal doorframes with doors that came absolutely complete.[25]

The importance of this meeting and Kahn's laboratory (the Alfred Newton Richards Medical Research Building) to Pearson's work at Middleton Parish Hall and Burne House is discussed in chapters five and six respectively.

Independence

As a private body, mostly of architects, receiving no public money and funded principally through its course fees, the AA enjoyed a high degree of independence. Around 1960, however, senior figures had proposed a merger with Imperial College, then part of the vast University of London. Negotiations took place over the following decade but by 1967 Pearson, then in his fourth year of teaching, was one of a number of staff who were voicing opposition to the plan. Already concerned at organisational changes by William Allen which he saw as increasingly bureaucratic ("You couldn't have a professor without a department, and then if you had a dean he had to have three or four professors each with departments....") and damaging to the AA's method of teaching, Pearson feared a merger would also provide an unnecessary safe haven for some via "security of tenure for senior personnel, which never existed at the AA as they could be fired at any time".[26]

ENCLOSURES FOR LEARNING

These programmes, together with some past school buildings and the present state of technology, not necessarily related to education, have created a climate in the United

Michael Pearson

Snack area at the SCSD El Dorado High School, Placentia. W. E. Blurock and Associates.

Photographs: Ronald Partridge.

JOURNAL OF THE UNIVERSITY OF MANCHESTER ARCHITECTURAL AND PLANNING SOCIETY

SUMMER 1955

244

NUMBER FOUR : SIGNIFICANT FORM

1/6

JOURNAL OF THE UNIVERSITY OF MANCHESTER ARCHITECTURAL AND PLANNING SOCIETY

244 Number 7

SPACE IN ARCHITECTURE:

THE VISUAL IMAGE OF ENVIRONMENT

WINTER 1956-7
PRICE 2.- or 30 cents

Photo: Picture Post Library.

Pearson discussed his concerns with his then year master Alvin Boyarsky, and with Boyarsky's support took the next step. Recalls Pearson, "I floated my ideas for getting rid of people who were keen to join Imperial College, and I went immediately to see David Allford, who was a Council member."[27]

The ultimate result was that Allen resigned and the merger—eventually, in 1970—was abandoned. Pearson is proud that, practically speaking, he "started the revolution that kept the AA private", although he left the AA shortly afterward, having been sacked by the new principal for disagreeing with certain of his actions. Pearson then taught for a period at the Bartlett.[28] He did, though, receive recognition for his efforts at the AA later, as will be seen.

Teaching II

In the summer of 1967, after canvassing a number of establishments in the United States and with the assistance of colleagues, Pearson was offered an appointment at the University of Oregon's school of architecture at Eugene for the fall term, teaching fifth year students. Head Bob Harris asked Pearson to "keep it lively" and "maintain whatever sense of connection to the rest of the world that may offset the cultural lag that could otherwise exist".[29]

Pearson found a passive, formal, unchallenging programme for students that "strangulated their creativity" and limited practicalities, whereas "At the AA, people would put something down [on paper] on the first day."[30] Additionally, they "forgot about the concept, […] they weren't very flexible in their thought, they weren't able to step aside and think around a problem".[31]

Opposite top
An article by Michael Pearson published in *Architectural Design*, May 1968.

Opposite bottom
244 was the address of three elegant stucco fronted town houses on Oxford Road, Manchester, serving as the School of Architecture. Sadly it was demolished to make way for a bleak students' union building. Michael Pearson, William Cowburn and Tony Travis created *244* as the Journal of the University of Manchester Architectural and Planning Society. That included doing everything, finally, down to collecting funds from advertisers to pay the printers. Most important it put them in touch with the 'bright young folk' in London.

Right
Michael Pearson was invited by Jim Richards, then editor of *The Architectural Review*, to search for new projects on the drawing board for a January issue called *Preview*, which included collecting and preparing material, writing brief texts which Richards later called "telegraphese", and graphic design of the issue.

THE ARCHITECTURAL REVIEW VOLUME CXXXI NUMBER 778 JANUARY 1962 FIVE SHILLINGS

Pearson injected some change, and secured talks on such subjects as lift development and American and Soviet approaches to providing breathable air for astronauts, but admits that "in my long hair and checked suit from Carnaby Street and [with] fluorescent green flowers on my silk shirt" he was perceived as "this young jerk [who] had come and started upsetting their applecart" by older members of the faculty.[32]

His measured frustration is clear from a reflective letter sent to Bob Harris the following spring, after leaving Eugene:

> Perhaps my main concern in the school was the barrier which seems to exist between staff and students and the reliance many placed on being told what to do. I think half of my time was spent breaking through this and coming to an understanding that we could operate and discuss a project as a two-way process on equal (or near equal) terms and not as a one-way offering.[33]

Research II

During his stay at Eugene, Pearson met architect Ezra Ehrenkrantz, originator of the School Construction Systems Development (SCSD) programme, and briefly taught with his partner Christopher Arnold. SCSD was a high quality, industrialised, economic, component-based approach to school provision allowing flexibility. Inspired by the comparable British Consortium of Local Authorities Special Programme (CLASP) of 1957, the prototype was erected at Stanford University, Palo Alto, California in 1964 and visited by Pearson.

Six subsystems comprised the SCSD specification: structure (excluding external walls, provided by the district architect), air conditioning (within the roof space and repositionable), lighting, partitions (fixed, demountable and openable), lockers and cupboards.

Commissioning echoed the burgeoning aerospace industry. A client gave performance goals for bidding suppliers to respond to with their versions of the subsystems, which therefore had to be compatible with each other or 'co-ordinated'. Innovatively, bids included maintenance for a period.

Pearson felt this concentration on a somewhat internalised environment with concomitant artificial support permitted "a deep plan form, single-storey factory shed" sensitive to the timebase of change, though he did recognise SCSD's limitations.[34]

He also found similarities in user need between such an 'enclosure for learning' and the *bürolandschaft* ("office landscaping" or "office community", known today as open plan) ideas developed in post-war Hamburg, implying that a structure designed in the right manner could function as either.[35] Pearson was planting a seed for his own future that would bloom at Burne House but find relevance initially in Lancaster.

Technology

Pearson's is not an overtly technological architecture, though this belies its inclusion where appropriate and a keen personal interest in the practical application of science. He also began to practice in one of the most charged periods of technological change since the late nineteenth century.[36]

Whilst at Eugene Pearson's unbridled but focused curiosity encompassed rapidly-assembled and mobile building shells; wider possibilities for air-supported volumes beyond fuel storage and temporary military buildings; Kaiser Permanente's first preventative medicine clinic; Skidmore, Owings & Merrill's plans for their low-rise headquarters for Weyerhaeuser, the first major American use of the *bürolandschaft*; and the RAND Corporation's work on office automation, hearing futurologist Olaf Helmer's predictions of a global electronic information network (fascinated, Pearson asked where this would be located— Helmer pointed to a wall socket and said "There!").[37]

Pearson categorically denies being influenced in any way by eccentric British group Archigram ('ARCHItecture' and 'teleGRAM'), established in 1961, and cheerfully optimistic regarding the positive social power of technology with their floating, walking, 'pod', 'plug-in' and 'instant' buildings, siding with Landau who believed the group was "stepping deeper and deeper and deeper into the shallows".[38]

And yet Pearson's extendible Crown Local Office buildings and enthusiasm for inflatable structures might be accounted similar to Archigram's belief that "You can roll out steel—any length. You can blow up a balloon—any size", and consciously or otherwise it is hard not to see something of Archigram's spirit finding its way into Pearson's Paris competition entries and changeable (plug-in?) cladding for Burne House.[39] Certainly the carwash-style rotating brush "floating up and down [the] tracks for the [...] window cleaning gondola" once discussed by Pearson and Allford as a possibility for the latter would have found favour with the group, though their enthusiasm eventually foundered over two practicalities: "what do you do with all this spray that comes off? Of course people get wet in the rain, but [...] and of course we couldn't solve the problem of the curved corners."[40]

Pearson also knew Archigrammers Dennis Crompton and, later, Warren Chalk. Architect Cedric Price, who was fascinated by lightweight, variable, interactive buildings and sympathised with Archigram in unrealised schemes and at London Zoo aviary, 1960–1963, designed with engineer Frank Newby and Anthony Armstrong-Jones (Lord Snowdon), and the Inter-Action Centre, Kentish Town, London, 1971–1977, also knew Allford and later joined Charles B Pearson & Son, working alongside Pearson in its pre-partnership days and becoming a life-long friend.

Ultimately, though, Pearson's interest in technology was—typically—used not for his own satisfaction but always in service of the brief, mediated by his working principles.

Leadership

In 1973 Pearson was voted president of the AA, which he sees as a direct result of his role in the earlier fight for the organisation's independence:

> I was a prime mover; there were a whole load of people talking about the situation and discussing it, and gaining superb publicity to alarm the Rector of Imperial College, but I took that action which resulted in Bill Allen resigning and therefore I was in line, once Imperial College had gone for good, for reward.[41]

The AA had by this time recovered from the difficult period following the abortive merger, with Boyarsky being elected to the new post of chairman and more democratic management structures set up. Pearson was able to report, towards the end of his term in office, that "The AA that now exists has been grabbed out of the dust and fashioned once more into a hot-bed of ideas..." and that "The AA now has the largest and most active student body it has ever had and perhaps the most important and impressive group of staff."[42]

1   MP, in conversation with the author, 9 July 2008.

2   MP, email to the author, 8 July 2008.

3-5   MP, in conversation with the author, 9 July 2008.

6   MP, in conversation with the author, 9 July 2008.

7   Fellow student Cowburn was two years older than
        Pearson but a period of National Service put him in
        the same year. He went on to work with Pearson on
        several projects after they both qualified.

8   MP, in conversation with the author, 9 July 2008. The
        reference is to Highpoint One, 1935, and Highpoint Two,
        1936–1938, by Tecton (a group of AA graduates) with
        Berthold Lubetkin.

9   MP, "Pearson's choice", Fred Hackworth, *Manchester
        Evening News*, 10 July 1973.

10   Eduardo Paolozzi, letter to MP, undated.

11   MP, in conversation with the author, 12 February
        2008.

12   By c. 1964, Pearson's address book included Gropius
        and Lubetkin, other architects such as Gerrit Rietveld
        (whose 1924 Schröder House Pearson visited in the
        company of Rietveld and his client, Truus Schröder)
        and Alison and Peter Smithson, sculptor Henry
        Moore, painter Patrick Heron, designer Robin Day and
        art historian Rudolf Wittkower; MP, in conversation with
        the author, 11 July 2008.

13   MP, in conversation with the author, 29 February 2008.

14   MP, "Michael Pearson AA President 1972–1974",
        AA Notes, January–February 1974, Architectural
        Association.

15   MP, in conversation with the author, 29 February 2008.

16   MP, email to Jim Helliwell, 25 April 2000.

17   MP, in conversation with the author, 27 March 2008.

18-24   Royston Landau, MP, "A note on an architecture of
        time", *Architectural Design*, August 1971.

25   MP, in conversation with the author, 12 February 2008.

26   MP, in conversation with the author, 2 September 2008.

27 & 28 MP, in conversation with the author, 1 March 2008

29   Robert Harris, letter to MP, 15 August 1967.

30   MP, in conversation with the author, 22 January
        2008 and MP, in conversation with the author,
        date unrecorded.

31 & 32 MP, in conversation with the author, 29 February 2008.

33   MP, letter to Robert Harris, 2 May 1968.

34   MP, "Enclosures for learning", *Architectural Design*,
        May 1968. Pearson distils the essence of his then-
        recent fact-finding and theorising into this piece.
        He anatomises any building by the lifespan of its
        components as a basis for his conclusions, noting
        that compared to the 50 year life of its structure,
        "Mechanical services may have a life of 12–15 years,
        lighting eight to 12 years, furnishings five to six years
        and decorations two to three years."

35   Frank Duffy, AA graduate and later co-founder of
        specialist office designers DEGW, was also looking into
        office landscaping at this time. Corresponding with
        Pearson, he noted "I haven't yet achieved a satisfactory
        definition of an office. Have you got one?" (Francis
        Duffy, letter to MP, undated but c. 1967).

36   Demonstration of a working laser, 1960, the first
        man in space and introduction of the contraceptive
        pill, 1961, and launch of the pioneering transatlantic
        communications satellite Telstar and first
        commercially viable hovercraft service, 1962, helped
        drive future prime minister Harold Wilson's famous
        1963 "white heat of technology" speech, with the
        remainder of the decade seeing in Britain alone the
        Post Office Tower microwave relay building, the TSR.2
        advanced prototype military jet and supersonic airliner
        Concorde and, worldwide, the first manned moon
        landing and rapid progress in computing.

37   A published paper resulted (MP, "Pneumatic
        Structures", *The Architectural Review*, October 1967),
        itself the subject of enquiries which Pearson fielded
        from Oregon; formed in the immediate aftermath
        of the Second World War as a privately owned but
        government-directed entity and later reconstituted as
        an independent non-profit body, RAND ('Research AND
        Development') originated many of the principles of
        office and personal computing, including interactive
        terminal-based systems and the packet switching
        basis of computer networks; MP, in conversation with
        the author, 22 January 2008

38   MP, in conversation with the author, 7 August 2008.
39   David Greene, *Archigram*, Issue 1, May 1961. In 1967 the
      Daily Telegraph invited Archigram to design a "house
      for the year 1990" to be exhibited in Harrods; the
      group's response included inflatable sleeping and
      seating structures.
40   MP, in conversation with the author, 1 March 2008.
41   MP, in conversation with the author, 2 September 2008.
42   MP, "The AA Now A report by the AA President Michael
      Pearson", *AA Notes*, January–February 1974, The
      Architectural Association.

4 | context

More than 20 years after winning the competition to design Scunthorpe Civic Centre, Charles E Pearson illustrated – beautifully – his heavily revised scheme. Note the pool adjacent to the main entrance, overlooked by a first floor balcony, the figures enjoying the view from the roof of the office wing and the outline of an extension to the left.

Charles B Pearson died in 1944. His highly successful career, latterly in partnership with his son, had seen the firm he had founded four decades previously flourish and gain a national presence. When Charles E Pearson was demobilised from the Royal Engineers in 1945 he reopened Charles B Pearson & Son as principal and determined to continue his father's work.

This should have proven difficult. Raw materials were rationed, building licences were required and government investment was concentrated on rehousing, initially using prefabricated structures, and restoring industry, both seldom requiring architects.

However, the newly-elected Labour government developed the wartime coalition's plans for educational change as represented by the Education Act 1944 and posited its own social reform programme based on the National Health Service Act 1946 ("the welfare state"). Simultaneously, a rapid increase in the birth rate occurred—the baby boom.

The outcome was a massive increase in the number of new schools and hospitals that would be needed, boosted by the 1959 Conservative government's specific pledge to increase the latter, and as has been seen, the firm's pre-war reputation had been established with just these building types as well as other civic works.

Opposite
The disciplined yet lively exterior
of Scunthorpe Civic Centre as
executed; view from the south
showing the council chamber
within the building's skeletal
frame, with the office wing behind.

Right
Present approach road to a well
preserved building.

Llandudno had given Charles E practical experience, relatively rare amongst his generation, of realising a large hospital scheme, whilst local co-incidence also played an appreciable part, as Michael Pearson recounts:

> They'd all been together at Lancashire County
> Council, I suppose in the 20s, and one of them
> who was there certainly was appointed chief
> architect of the North West Regional Hospital
> Board and he said to father there's plenty of work
> for you to do but you'll have to open an office
> in Manchester, so he opened the office with
> a fellow who'd trained as a pupil in Lancaster
> before the war and he had one or two other
> ex-pupils who came to work for him.[1]

The Lancaster architect who opened this second office in March 1949 was George Ronald Lovell. Slightly younger than Charles E, he had also served with the Royal Engineers and worked on a wide range of military projects and was articled to both Charles E and Charles B.

The firm was thus better placed than many and two projects in particular—one a link to the past, the other a foretaste of the future—signalled that its success would continue, although the question of whether the momentum of the shift toward modernism, signposted before the war with Scunthorpe Civic Centre, was now unstoppable, would remain unanswered for a little longer.

In 1955 Charles E, along with Dennis Burneside, began to redesign Scunthorpe for a new site and in a radically different idiom. Nothing of the 1937 plan survived. Instead a long, narrow, five-storey block of offices formed a right angle with a shorter, lower, wider wing whose slate-clad steel frame was left open to the south, forming a cage for the horseshoe-shaped double-height council chamber nestling within. Interiors featured abundant glazing, mezzanines and a minimalist main stair. Only the emphatic brick-clad towers at either end of the office wing, acting as stops for the runs of glazing, retained a faint echo of the pre-war scheme and its possible sources. In their material, massing and slit windows, these evoke Dudok's acclaimed Hilversum Town Hall, 1924–1930.

Though its arrangement of simple forms and opposition of solidity and openness may be grounded in pre-war Modernists such as Le Corbusier, the scheme as built was an original composition and a remarkable declaration of Charles E's enthusiasm for the new 'International Style'. A considered, restricted palette of materials contributed to the refinement typical of this architecture but also of his father's works. Sensitivity to location continued through the installation of a large panel of Roman mosaic pavement recovered from archaeological excavations at nearby Winterton.

Left
The building in its gentle
landscape today.

Right
The Romano-British mosaic
in all its glory.

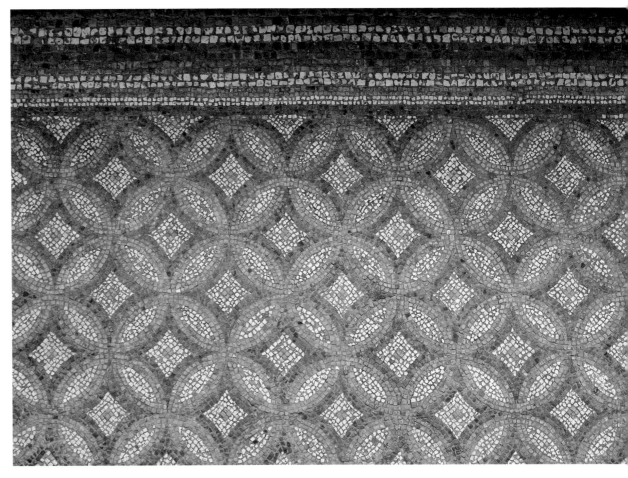

Still in use today as Pittwood House, home of
North Lincolnshire Council, and Grade II listed, English
Heritage recently praised Charles E's building for its
"open planning, subtle spatial effects and interesting
materials and artifacts" and stressed its progressive
aspect, describing it as "deliberately modern".[2] This is
intriguing in light of other contemporaneous work by
the practice, as will be seen.

The second project was directly attributable
to the new climate—design and construction of
West Cumberland Hospital at Whitehaven, 80–100
miles northwest of Lancaster along the coast. Also
begun in 1955, this was one of the first of the new
district general hospitals and came to Pearson as a
direct result of his previous experience in the field.
The job—by far the firm's largest, having a value
of around £50 million today and taking ten years to
complete—allowed the ideas set out at Llandudno
to be expanded whilst also looking to Swedish
practice for ideas (the district general hospital
concept itself had American roots, especially in its
later incarnations).

Top
West Cumberland Hospital.
Typical ward plan based upon
earlier Scandinavian examples.

Opposite
Looking back over the main
access road with more planting
than parking.

Barnsley District General
Hospital commissioned from
the practice after its success
being highly commended in the
Boston hospital competition.
View northeast from junction of
Summer Lane and Pogmoor Road:
maternity department on the
left and psychiatric department
beyond right.

Pearson was assisted by Peter Pearson Lund, his nephew, who had joined in 1951 and shared an architectural and military engineering background with his uncle and colleagues.

This commission, along with second prize for the 1960 University of Wales teaching hospital Cardiff competition and a 'highly commended' for Boston Hospital, Lincolnshire, led to the series of built hospitals for which the firm became well-known. These included Sharoe Green, Preston, 1955–1968, St Helen district general, Barnsley (scheme 1961) and Preston district general (scheme 1965) and Kilton hospital, Worksop (scheme 1974).

Insight into Pearson's planning skill, which his son would take further, can be gained by examining the Cardiff scheme briefly. To foster co-operation and prevent "a detached academic attitude of mind", teaching and clinical staff were co-located.[3] Considerable thought was given to the disposition of wards for both sunlight and views. 'Layers' of circulation separated people and services: at the lowest level, a corridor handled waste; supplies were distributed on the next; ground floor entrances split patients into ambulant, vehicle-conveyed, and so on; the final layer of theatres and support areas was entirely clinical.

One last job from this period should be noted, as its gestation and realisation summarise the post-war ideological opposition in architecture which Charles E still had to work within and its impact on the firm.

In 1957 Lovell's and Michael Sharp's competition entry for Carlisle Civic Centre won first prize. A ten-storey tower housed offices to the north of the site. Attached and spreading south was a two-storey block for the civic suite; from its second floor ran a link to the council chamber, a detached three-storey octagon raised above an open ground floor arcade. This striking arrangement, with its "informal yet dignified massing and changing of plane of facade", won praise:

The disposition of these separate units is excellent [...] The tower block will be an interesting feature viewed when entering Carlisle from the north [and] detachment of the council chamber enables the designer to give expression to and emphasise the importance of the chamber as the dominant feature in the layout.[4]

The mix of materials was also noted, aluminium and copper contrasting with rubble walling on walls and ground floor spandrel panels. The assessor felt this

while being a positive step forward in design and a dignified essay in the contemporary manner, will also harmonise admirably with and indeed pay tribute to the marked local characteristics of Carlisle.[5]

But this opinion was not shared by the architectural press, The Architects' Journal pointedly criticising the council chamber as a "quaint folly" and a "not-quite-contemporary edifice".[6] This may explain the major change between competition and construction—omission of the rubble wall cladding and the Tudor apexes to the council chamber roof.

A remarkably clean, almost chaste look resulted, especially in the precise but filigree tower summit through continuation of the concrete framework over its rooftop plant. Interiors were a similar mix of pre-war craft tradition and sometimes startling post-war modernity.

From this point on, despite individual architects' own views and an evolving management situation (see List of projects and information on sources), both of which might be thought to have militated against anything that could be called a house style, the firm sustained a degree of visual coherence across much of its post-war output which maintained the Pearsons' pre-war affinities for materials yet folded this into a confirmed modernism.

Cumberland Infirmary, Carlisle, two 30 bed wards per floor around a six storey courtyard over a diagnostic and treatment podium. The link corridor to the existing hospital is visible on the left.

Kilton Hospital, Worksop: a later
courtyard scheme designed around
NHS 'Nucleus' standard L-shape
constraints, not always suitable for
planning all types of department.

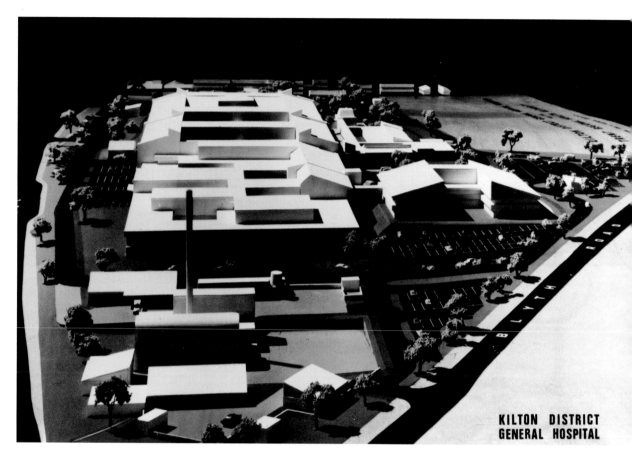

KILTON DISTRICT
GENERAL HOSPITAL

Ripley school gymnasium, left, and classroom blocks. The original school buildings were altered by Charles E Pearson after war damage.

...vations of the winning Carlisle
...ic Centre scheme, showing the
...nacular treatment of the lower
...ors and the octagonal council
...mber which pleased the assessor
...c exercised Astragal. The separate
...embly hall was to be constructed
...en funds allowed.

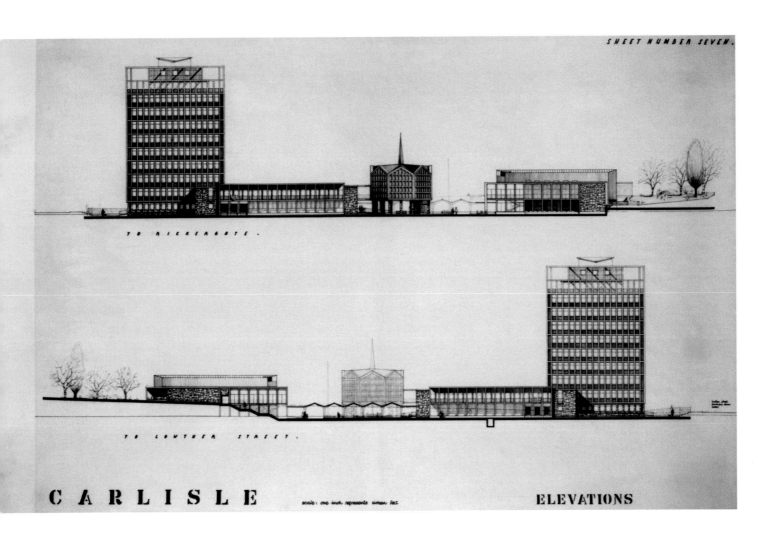

CARLISLE   scale: one inch represents sixteen feet   ELEVATIONS

Carlisle Civic Centre,
reception room.

Thus at Sharoe Green (Lovell and Sharp), box balconies and asymmetric stair towers of unpainted board-marked concrete set up a rich textural dialogue as well as animating the elevations. In Lancaster town centre, the near-windowless sandstone box of the Masonic Hall extension of 1959–1961 (John Stephenson) is a cool exercise in volume and planes and at Ripley school the new gymnasium by Geoff Leather, designed as late as 1969, features cladding that refers closely to the stonework of the adjacent late Victorian Gothic Revival chapel by Hubert J Austin but also a dramatic, side-glazed roof of zig-zag profile.

It was within this softer version of Modernism, tempered as it was by the strong rooting of the firm's founders, history and practitioners in their locality and the weight of built work accrued in that locality, which Michael Pearson, aged 25 and recently qualified, would have to make his mark.

1   MP, in conversation with the author, 29 February 2008.

2   Law and Government Buildings Selection Guide, English Heritage, March 2007.

3   "Extract from the Second prize-winners report", *The Architect and Building News*, 8 June 1960.

4 & 5   Winner's report, "Winning design for Carlisle's municipal building", *The Architects' Journal*, 15 August 1957; Assessor's report, Winning design for Carlisle's municipal building, *The Architect and Building News*.

6   "The Living and The Dead", *The Architects' Journal*; "Astragal", *The Architects' Journal*.

5 | British Works

Michael Pearson was teaching
at the Architectural Association
School of Architecture in
the 1960s. He later joined the
AA Council and was elected
president in 1973.

In 1958, after working at Richard Sheppard and Partners
for a year on construction defects and door frame
details for a new hall of residence, Michael Pearson
opened a London office for Charles B Pearson & Son
at Wimpole Street, Marylebone with Bill Cowburn.
Though a method of gaining a useful presence in
the capital, Pearson himself gives an additional
explanation clearly linked to his time at university:

> I was the rat who got on the train to Euston
> with a one-way ticket when I'd finished at
> Manchester [...] I felt I'd done everything I
> could do in Manchester, and 75 per cent of the
> architects in the country were in London, all
> the bright boys were there, and I wanted to be
> where people were thinking seriously about
> the direction of architecture.[1]

Although Pearson's inaugural tasks for his father's
firm were indeed in London – work on service stations
for National Benzole with Cedric Price, who had by
then joined Charles E Pearson from Fry Drew – all
but one of Pearson's major projects in his first ten
years ended up firmly localised in Lancashire since,
as Pearson admits, "we weren't getting any work
in London – nobody told me how to get work".[2]
They do, though, reveal the point of origin of each
of Pearson's major concerns in architecture, namely
user need, flexibility, service provision and a building's
relationship with its surroundings, with the last of
them – significantly, perhaps, the only one actually
to be located in the south of England – beginning
to illustrate the power of process for Pearson in the
evolution of a design.

The first, in 1959, contains tantalising hints of what
was to come. At Lindow Square, a tight grid of Victorian
housing in central Lancaster, Price was the lead architect
preparing working drawings for two small blocks of
almshouses for the elderly. Of simple arrangement
themselves, each block having a double pitched roof on
a rectilinear plan, the natural slope of the site was the
key to enlivening the scheme as it allowed, for the
western-most block, a front door onto the street but a
two-storey rear aspect with accompanying views. The
eastern block, being at the lower end of the slope, was
single-storey throughout. Extensive glazing, balconies
and traditional stone end walls featured.

Pearson's small but important contribution was
to the landscaping, locating bench seats and individual
planting beds by residents' doors and selectively
lowering the high boundary walls in places to create
little views and vistas out of the site at convenient
heights for residents when walking around their
gardens or the ground floors of their houses.

Quips Pearson, of his work with Price here, "He
did the windows, I did the walls", though this plays
down its importance.[3] Close concern for users and
the intricate shaping of the edges of a building
where it joins its immediate environs are detectable
throughout Pearson's work and it is fascinating to find
them first displayed here.

For Pearson's next work, the small part of a larger
whole was more substantial, and he seized upon it to
extend his reach in the areas that were important to him.

In 1956 the practice was commissioned to design
two new buildings for Lancaster Royal Grammar
School on part of its magnificent hill site overlooking
the city, a chemistry block and a dining hall. At the
latter, and taking full advantage of the location, the
seating area was raised above a plinth housing
the boiler and toilets and placed in a deeply glazed
storey crowned with a butterfly roof with clerestory
windows. Pearson describes his involvement as "minor
tinkering down there, really, which I hope altered the
architectural character from a rather sterile little box
to one with a bit of life".[4]

By "down there", Pearson means the two entrances
to the hall. Creating an appropriate progression from
the north door through the narrow, dark corridor

onto which it opened to the bright hall above began with inserting a "random pattern of little slots" in the corridor wall to give glimpses outside.[5] This is clearly a development of Pearson's work at Lindow Square but he volunteers the influence of Le Corbusier's twinned Maisons Jaoul houses, 1952–1954, and James Stirling, who had taken a similar approach with the fenestration of his contemporaneous Langham House Close flats at Ham Common, Richmond-upon-Thames (with James Gowan) and who in turn admired Le Corbusier. Stirling and Gowan's flats became a model which Pearson was to return to later.

Where the west entrance joins the corridor, Pearson combined spatial manipulation with the breaking of the plane of the exterior. A dog-leg stair is rotated away from the obvious alignment and pushed forward of the building line in a semi-glazed box; critically, the glazing around its upper flights extends slightly lower than that of the main hall to provide anticipatory views:

> I turned this stair through 180 degrees [perpendicular to the building and corridor axes] so you come up here, and on a lovely day you can see right across Morecambe Bay before you turn again and go into the big space.[6]

The experience is completed by the user being then free to make a further turn, recapturing the same westerly view but more expansively (and which, before nearly 50 years of tree growth, took in Lancaster castle and the priory church). In this context, Pearson also worked on a landscaping scheme here, where a new route from the existing school to the new site was planned. This included an arboretum with avenues for views to the Victorian cathedral church of St Peter, by Lancaster architect Edward Paley, which is a focal point in views from the dining hall. Again, Pearson's work at the school was to sow seeds for the future; afterwards, he almost always included planting in his schemes.

Back at ground level, Pearson applied the same care to how buildings met the land as he had at the almshouses through what would become another signature – a love of materials. The plinth was robustly stone-finished in response to the dominant material locally; a nicely curved wall adjacent to the north door, counterbalancing the building's angular lines but also disguising the dustbin store, is executed in deeply-split stone with a strongly tactile quality. At the west entrance, marking its importance

in the original arboretum scheme, an agreeable mix of materials is used – cobbles at path edges, thin flint-rich concrete plates lining the Corbusian 'slots' and the firm's favourite board-marked concrete for the walls of the stair box. This use of natural, durable materials that are pleasing to the eye and the hand is another similarity with Stirling and Gowan and Le Corbusier's then-current housing projects.

The attention to detail and the user experience shown by Pearson at his – and his father's – former school make a real impression even today, as new generations of pupils rush through and around the building. Wonderfully appropriately, his 'slots' are arranged at various heights and thus accommodate observers of a similar range.

Pearson states that the school "certainly launched me into the next range of designs".[7] The first of these was another whose outline had already been decided, but the scale increased once more and enabled Pearson to explore the possibilities of materials again and self-confidently – almost cheekily – mix stylistic sources to dramatic effect.

Shackcliffe Green School at Moston in Greater Manchester came to the London office in 1960 part-formed, as a diagrammatic plan which had been

Below and opposite bottom
Block plan of the Shackcliffe
Green scheme and plans of the
ground floor and upper levels
of the four-storey general
classroom block.

Opposite top
The Miesian boiler room and
kitchen block with the upper
parts of the assembly hall visible
beyond the chimney.

Opposite middle
The Japanese-influenced
general classroom block of
Shackcliffe Green school; facades
retain visual interest despite
the extremely attenuated
material palette.

put forward to release the money – the linked
corridor and the four-storey block and the two
halls were determined when I came into the project,
but we did that [design] from that point of really
a block plan [...] which set out the relationship of
the volumes. We had a four-storey block of science
laboratories and classrooms, and then the central
spine was mainly administrative.[8]

It was the visual statement that such a plan might
permit which inspired Pearson; by his own admission,
appearance was a primary stimulus for his design. So
the general classroom block, the tallest on the site,

... was totally influenced by [a] building done by
the great architect of the time and illustrated
in Japan Architect [...] a town hall built of pre-
cast concrete blocks that were really quite big
– but it was the visual imagery of what he was
doing that we rather liked; the proportion of the

windows and the fact that the windows were
divided into three horizontal panes [...] so you
get this very horizontal emphasis, and quite long
slots for the windows between the structural
columns. [Also we] certainly did do a lot of work
with the golden section, in looking for suitable
proportions generally.[9]

The Japanese effect was aided by thin-section metal
window frames set back from the visually massive
reinforced concrete structural beams and columns,
and omission of the latter at corners. This adoption/
adaptation of a wholly foreign vision, whilst entirely
valid in itself, can also be seen as a neat sidestepping
of the argument, permeating post-war British
architecture at the time, between 'pure' Modernism,
as expressed in Britain by what critic Reyner Banham –
who also promoted technology in architecture –
called the New Brutalism, or the lighter, looser

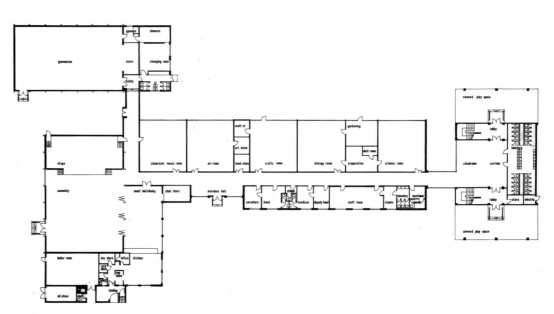

form which historian Nikolaus Pevsner and critic JM Richards, editing *The Architectural Review* (to which Pearson would contribute and whose January Preview section, showcasing new work by British practitioners, he would guest edit, write and lay out in 1961 and 1962), dubbed the New Humanism. Pearson also regards the concrete block walls as deriving from his 1962 research visit to the United States.

For the halls and specialist classrooms, the need for large unobstructed spans required steel and drove the aesthetic in an entirely different direction. Pearson cheerfully admits to copying Alison and Peter Smithson's hugely influential Hunstanton school, Norfolk (1954) when searching for a solution. He equally honestly recalls the problem this caused:

> We put the steel on the outside... and had a great deal of difficulty waterproofing it! You put the steel on the outside and you've got to fix the enclosure of the room to the steel; well, you have to waterproof these fixings [...] It's a perverse way of doing it – it's easier to put the steel inside and have the waterproof membrane round the outside.[10]

Other architects had of course favoured exposed steel, not least Ludwig Mies van der Rohe at the Illinois Institute of Technology's Crown Hall, Chicago (1950-1956, but published in Britain in 1948); Pearson himself cites the Chicago Civic Centre by Jacques Brownson of CF Murphy Associates (and others), begun in 1960, as another specific source.

Shackcliffe has similarities with other British educational architecture of the time, not least Yorke Rosenberg Mardall's High Park School, Stourbridge, 1959, but with the contrast of mass and transparency resulting from his choices Pearson formed an arresting grouping, beginning an awareness of how the visual elements of a design could work on a large as well as small scale, something he would display much later at Burne House.

Top left
Unfinished concrete, in block and poured forms, contribute to the aesthetic and reduce maintenance costs.

Bottom
Detail of exposed steel member junctions.

Top right
Classroom interior displaying unequal window pane sizes in each sub-bay.

Pearson though thinks the blockwork the least inspired, "weakest part" of Shackcliffe.[11] He ruefully accepts that it taught a practical lesson, namely the incompatibility of exposed concrete and British weather, but drolly describes Shackcliffe as his 'Mies and Japanese' work.

Pearson's Shackcliffe buildings survive as the core of North Manchester High School for Girls – appropriately, given Pearson's own scholastic enthusiasms, a specialist science college. The blocks have received new aluminium roofs, pitched in the case of the general classroom block where glazing of a new pattern has replaced the distinctive facades Pearson created 40 years ago. The gymnasium remains in use, although the assembly hall, in truly adaptable fashion, is now given over exclusively to dining.

At a time when aged school buildings, in particular, are under pressure to be radically remodelled or demolished, this resilience is a testament to the effectiveness of Pearson's work.

Only in his next commission, begun at the same time as Shackcliffe but completed before it, did Pearson enjoy complete design freedom from the outset. Though geographically remote and modest in scope, the ambition it betrays, the inspiration it drew from and the relevance it holds for Pearson's later architecture make it an important part of the story.

About five miles west of Lancaster on the outskirts of the large coastal village of Heysham lies the smaller village of Middleton. In 1960, Pearson's London office was given the job of designing the new Middleton parish hall.

The location chosen was at the eastern edge of the green, on a slope looking out onto open fields. Given this, the initial surprise is the form which Pearson's building took; although the character of the existing buildings is one of domestic, vernacular housing, the hall is a flat-roofed, double-height, concrete block box with prominent glazing, especially to the east where it appears as two continuous vertical bays.

However, Pearson was not being quite so cavalier with the hall's image-in-context as this bald description suggests. The natural slope of the site reduces the impact of the building when seen from the village side, lowering it to a single storey on the entrance facade, and familiar materials are once again deployed to soften, including wood strip cladding to roof edges and window lintels and bullnose brick for window sills. The hall is finished in painted render to match the nearby houses. Visually

striking, the real interest is in its servicing and how this relates to its plan.

To fulfil the brief for a large open area which could be used as flexibly as possible, Pearson began with the structure. Because of their height and the need for a column-free interior, the walls needed strengthening, especially on the east facade with its two large floor-to-ceiling windows with doors. This was achieved by building in multiple returns, removing the need for additional support. As Pearson says, "They're buttresses, if you like", and this applies to their visual appearance as well as their structural function.[12]

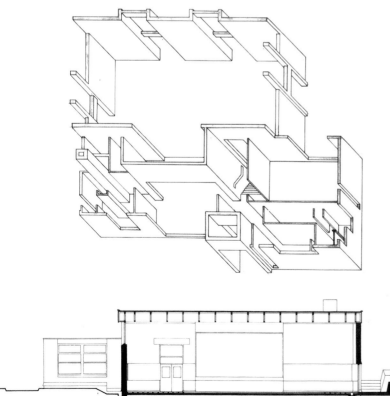

Services could now be introduced, and here Pearson turned for inspiration to the man whose work in this area appealed and who he would meet in two years' time – Louis Kahn.

Born in 1901, Kahn rapidly developed an architecture informed by a reverence for mass but also by his self-coined concept of 'served' and 'servant' spaces; respectively, spaces occupied by people or the core function of a building and spaces occupied by the services needed to allow that core function to operate – lifts, stairs, utility ducts. Kahn's first real evocation of this concept was at the Alfred Newton Richards Medical Research Building at the University of Pennsylvania, Philadelphia, the laboratory Pearson visited whilst on his 1962 trip but which had been started in 1957. In an acknowledged debt to Frank Lloyd Wright's now-lost Larkin administration building, New York, of 1904, services are clustered at the edge of the research blocks but in brick towers set against glazed laboratories, drawing separate but equal attention to those services and the spaces they supply.

At Middleton, Pearson is clear: "The principal concerns were to try and adopt Louis Kahn's serviced and service spaces", something which would also be revisited at Burne House.[13]

The folded wall structure contributed by providing space for heating, cabling and so on. Examining the axonometric of the hall reproduced in this chapter, Pearson points out his 'service', or servant, spaces and bays:

> That's got the water tank in it, [...] this is a sort of service space, the stage, and some of these had cupboards in them[;] electric cables ran up in those spaces, for instance, and then distributed out so the walls were kept clear. That was the intention.[14]

As at Shackcliffe, the boiler and kitchen were placed in smaller, lower attached blocks on the village side of the hall, tempering its single large mass with variable lesser masses, a square-section brick

Above
Middleton parish hall interior,
showing the stage.

Opposite
Mayford approved school from
the northwest.

chimney acting almost as a sculptural feature and
adding further domesticity.

With Middleton, therefore, Pearson succeeded
in creating a structure which – Kahnian services,
wide-spanning roof and all – resembles a minimalist,
functional, industrial shed under the skin but which in
finish and in operation is the homely, useful, adaptable
building required. Today, the hall sits remarkably well
in the landscape with its wood trim now silvered and
with more houses now clustered around it. Nicely, in
producing a new village hall for a new age, Pearson
was following in family footsteps.

Middleton was finished in 1963, Shackcliffe in
1965. Pearson continued to teach at the AA whilst
running the London office, and the same year that
Shackcliffe was completed saw Pearson receive
a commission which would enable him to enact
theories of adaptability provision and user/client
need in even more depth. Seminally, it was also a
commission whose end result represents the first
objectively analysable example of the notion of
'process' in his work, of the iterative reconsideration
of a design by client and architect and the results that
this can achieve, and so Pearson's thoughts on this
project are quoted in some detail. Even the unusually

casual manner in which the commission arrived
begins another minor theme of his working life:

> You know that was extraordinary; I was sitting
> wherever I was sitting, wondering what I was
> to do in the coming weeks, apart from doing
> this journalism at The Review and teaching at
> the AA, and I got this telephone call from an
> architect at the LCC and he said do I have enough
> time to consider designing a new approved
> school for them?[15]

Approved schools were established in 1933 and were
run by local authorities. They received juveniles from
mainstream schools when behavioural problems
arose or from courts as sentences for minor crimes
(more serious cases were referred to borstals).
Many were old reformatories and industrial schools
renamed, but the offer to Pearson was to design
Mayford approved school, a wholly new residential
establishment in Mayford, just outside Woking in
Surrey. The scheme called for accommodation for a
planned total of 150 boys on a mature parkland site
adjacent to existing school facilities.

For Pearson the first step was to consider the
fundamental question of how the boys should be
housed. The obvious – because cheapest – and expected
solution was a single slab block for all, but Pearson
was not convinced and felt that breaking the boys up
into groups, in separate buildings, would yield benefits
"on the basis that smaller communities give a better
exchange than larger communities".[16] Pearson explains:

> I think one's duty as an architect is always to
> challenge the brief. Somebody had set it up on
> some notional idea and I challenged it on the
> basis of the sociology of the place, really, which
> led to the architecture, as it always should.[17]

In the very special case of Mayford, the architecture
was also trying to drive behaviour.

At this juncture the importance of the relationship between architect and client becomes apparent. Chairman of the client body committee was Methodist minister and Socialist campaigner Donald Soper, later Lord Soper. As Pearson describes it:

> He was incredible; very bright, intelligent, and sympathetic to everything I said. Not outrageously critical but critical, at the same time, as one has to be.[18]

Soper accepted Pearson's concept of separation, freeing Pearson to work on the next level of detail – the nature and placement of the individual blocks, where

> the argument was, do you put them all together, do you create houses, like a lot of schools have, and I created three or four houses and thought that it was important that they walked to school, not a huge distance, but that they had to walk from one end of the site to the other, and there were to be three of these houses and two units within each, which were joined by a kitchen and dining room.[19]

Further discussion took place over the number and size of the boys' bedrooms within the units:

> They argued that they couldn't have two boys in a room, they couldn't afford individual rooms, four seemed like too many – two could gang up against two [...].[20]

Ultimately a mix of single- and four-bed rooms was settled on, sleeping 15 boys in total per unit, arranged in an L-shape.

> We tried to make all the [boys'] rooms different if we could, and we explored the ratio of length to breadth in terms of what gave the maximum number of variations of layout, because they [only] had a bed and they had a bedside cupboard and they had wall space.[21] [...] Room shapes were designed to allow the maximum variations for boys to personalise their base.[22]

Quarters for the house master and other staff completed a square around a central stair. Neatly, the door of the house master's bedroom was placed so as to give a direct view of all the boys' doors.

Flexibility – that is, adaptability – was included, and not just for staff, whose rooms had interconnecting doors and so could be combined or kept separate as needed. The boys' sitting, common and dining rooms

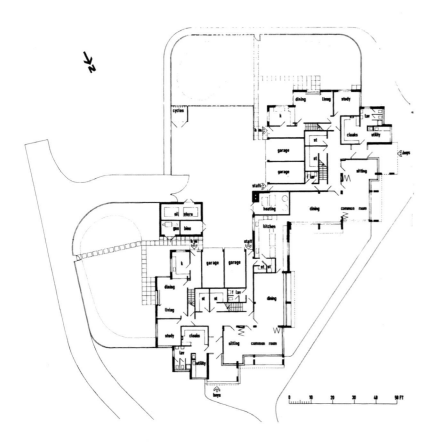

also had sliding doors between them so that the available space could be adjusted for different activities as needed. Each self-contained unit would also contain living rooms for staff, studies and garages as well as the expected plant and service areas.

In execution these units would be paired, for a total of 30 boys in each house building. Although abandonment of the single slab approach had the additional benefit of greatly reducing the monotony associated with institutional buildings, care was still taken to break up the mass of even these two-storey blocks. Helpfully this could be partly achieved simply by reflecting the plan in the external appearance, variation in room shape, size and views (which are available to all points of the compass, shared between staff and boys) driving a relaxed, irregular elevational treatment.

Initial construction in March 1965 was limited to the first block only, named Churchill House. The engineering fell to Frank Newby of Felix J Samuley and Partners. Newby and Pearson collaborated on a structural scheme to permit the required degree of openness in the facades and allowance for change within, using load-bearing crosswalls to bring freedom to the placement of other components and allow Pearson to "play with space and form", sometimes a little whimsically.[23] Outside, for example, narrow brick piers separated slightly from the walls nominally supported the overhanging first floor but were in fact structurally unnecessary, deep-span reinforced concrete beams performing this function. The piers did, though, form a visual link with the rest of the building, since the 'slots' they created – themselves reminiscent of Lindow Square and Lancaster Royal Grammar School – harmonised with the fenestration, a pattern of horizontal and vertical areas of glazing that reflects both Le Corbusier's Maisons Jaoul and Stirling and Gowan's Ham Common flats.

Pearson's trademark sculptural flue also appeared, and the honest use of simple but high-quality, largely

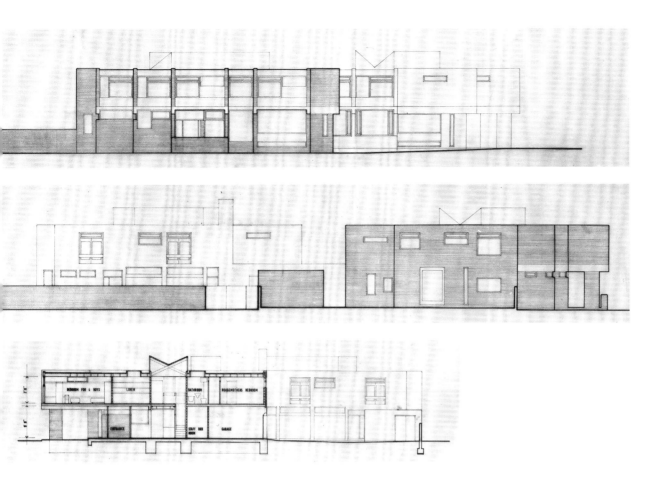

self-finished, materials – brick, concrete, wood, fibrous cement panels – fitted with Pearson's emerging aesthetic sense and the buildings of the surrounding area. This also represented a practical response to another element of the brief, being resistant to damage and long-lasting. Landscaping was included.

Mayford was completed in June 1966. Over the years, the flexibility included by Pearson proved valuable, its rooms being used "in a variety of ways which were not envisaged in the original brief".[24] The forbidding and drab nature expected of an establishment building designed for the most serious of purposes was exchanged for a humane and welcoming experience. Pearson's renunciation of a single large building in favour of multiple, small units, with well-detailed facades in good materials, rendered Mayford more akin to private housing and thus endeavoured to see that boys were treated, and would regard themselves, as individuals. That this perhaps succeeded can be judged from the following:

Sports day was interesting when former offenders came back to their old school.[25] [...] All these old inmates used to come back

because it was their school, their college, their community, their social scene.[26]

Moreover, basic elements of Pearson's architecture – in-built capacity for change, sensitivity to a building's environment, consideration of client and user need and the engagement and refinement process around this, teasing out solutions by the exchange of ideas – coalesced, thanks to a committed practitioner and "a most enlightened client".[27]

Changes in socio-political theory meant no further house blocks were built and approved schools themselves were abolished in the late 1960s. Churchill House itself, which assumed a variety of uses subsequently, was demolished in 2005/2006, before research for the present work began. The link with particular educational provision has been sustained, however, as a council school for children with autistic spectrum disorders moved to its new building on the site in time for the autumn term of 2007.

For Pearson, these five projects represent a progression of his "attitude towards design and objectives and aspirations in terms of what kind of image are you

projecting to the world".[28] In them, too, the threads of
his interests – in users, in adaptability, in services, in
surroundings – can be seen to grow, intertwine and
converge, producing architecture with a logic and a
lasting value, qualities which would be projected into
later schemes.

Taken together, they form a confident introduction
to Pearson's early British work.

In quick succession now, two built works and
two unbuilt designs would allow Pearson to take the
next steps toward realising a full architectural vision,
a path that would culminate with Burne House. They
are presented here slightly out of sequence in order
to more clearly track their pertinence to that building,
although the continuation of Pearson's beliefs can be
traced within them as individual projects.

In 1969 Charles B Pearson Son & Partners were
engaged to upgrade a school on the edge of Bolton
in Lancashire. Pearson was asked by Raymond Price,

job architect, to assist by designing one of its major
components. In taking on Turton school swimming
pool, Pearson was able to demonstrate that his
facility for using materials for visual effect, shown
at Shackcliffe Green, and real awareness of structure,
displayed at Middleton and Mayford, could be taken
in a new direction for synergistic effect.

The principal consideration was the containment
of the pool, both structurally (as a high-ceilinged,
essentially single-storey, building) and architecturally.
Consensus amongst Pearson's contemporaries was
elusive; at Coventry, steel columns supported the roof
of the city architect's department's new Central Baths
(completed 1966) and enabled the entire south wall
to be of glass, in keeping with the war-shredded city's
heartfelt attempt to create openness and transparency
out of darkness and loss. Conversely at his pool in Swiss
Cottage, London of 1964, Basil Spence favoured stone-
faced walls only partly relieved by slatted windows.

To address both points and the brief, Pearson was attracted by the possibility of using a masonry diaphragm wall which comprises two parallel walls tied together by cross-walls to form a rigid matrix. It has high strength but relatively low weight per unit of area, making foundation construction cheaper and quicker. If brick, a wholly traditional material for schools, was used as the raw material, a very attractive and appropriate architectural finish could result without further work. Advantages of cost also accrue since only one trade is involved. Remembers Pearson:

> I think this had been floating around as a theory and probably used elsewhere but I was rather taken by the idea of this very deep wall so you've got enormous lateral stability.[29]

Pearson therefore originated an extremely precisely thought-out plan based entirely around the dimensions of a then-standard brick, namely 4½ x 9".[30] The two parallel walls are each a single brick width thick and are 3' 9" (a multiple of the brick length) apart, tied together by cross-walls of the same thickness placed at 3' 9" centres. This forms the cellular construction typical of a masonry diaphragm wall, whose effective overall width in this instance is therefore around 4' 6".

Externally, vertical piers or buttresses exactly one brick length wide, spaced to create bays of two different sizes grouped in the pattern AB BA BB, etc. along the main facade, appear to be representations of the cross-walls. However, displaying the whimsy seen at Mayford, these are in fact of no structural value; they do not coincide with every cross-wall and specifically do not support the roof at the building's corners (concrete beams are used for this). Pearson's aim was simply to create

> a kind of decorative effect [from] classical architecture. It's got the proportions of a Renaissance or Roman temple.[31]

posite

terior. The viewing gallery
created by penetrations in
e north wall around the walls
pporting the roof beams.
ly one narrow window in
ternal walls to minimise
are whilst swimming.

low

n axonometric, sketched by
arson during discussion
r the present work, of the
asonry diaphragm wall
ncept employed at Turton.

If these piers can be read as pilasters, the building's projecting roof and chamfered plinth serve as their capitals and bases.

The only window in the entire structure is a single penetration in the west end wall at its junction with the south wall, narrow but running the entire height of the building. Regarding the pool surface, Pearson was insistent there be

> *no* windows at this level – *everyone* does windows and they all produce reflection [...] There is a window [...] and that illuminates the wall, this wall inside; we were particular in wanting to have just a peep in to see what's going on – you know, you can see it's a swimming pool – and no [other] windows [...] obviously

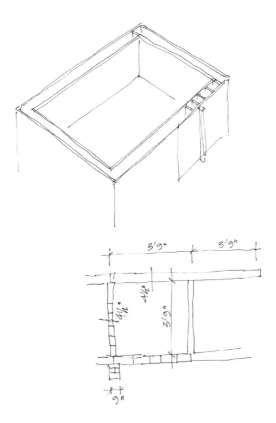

people criticised it for not having any windows... I can understand that, but they didn't realise that if you've got windows here you can't very often see the surface of the water [when swimming] except right in front of you, you get the reflection of the whole thing and it's very debilitating.[32]

Eminently logical, this is of course also a continuation of Pearson's predilection for 'slots', whilst the site perimeter features lowered walls, as used at Lindow Square. A translucent fibreglass roof provided most of the natural light, supported on concrete beams. These rest on free-standing, load-bearing brick walls to the north to enable the formation of a first-floor spectators' gallery. Changing rooms and ancillary services are located in a low-rise block to the north.

The whole is a remarkably sophisticated exercise, producing a building whose structure is its architecture and vice versa. It is powerfully but not aggressively modelled, the external piers or pilasters setting up a powerful visual rhythm and contributing greatly to the building's distinctive sculptural presence in the landscape. As with Shackcliffe the pool remains in use, as part of what is now Turton High School Media Arts College, although it and the other school buildings were re-roofed around 2005.

In the same year that he received the Turton job, a cliché of co-incidence – the chance meeting in a pub – led to Pearson's smallest new building that, size notwithstanding, is also one of his most fascinating projects. Clearly demonstrating every Pearson principle despite the extremely restricted scale, the Ewen studio addition essays allowance for change, relatively complex services and sensitivity for the surrounding environment in just 40 square metres. Total collaboration with the client, who in this instance was also the end user, to ensure his needs were fully addressed is also evident, arguably to a greater degree than in any of Pearson's completed

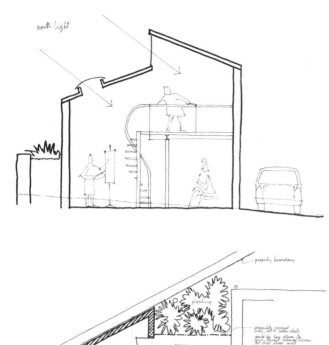

north light

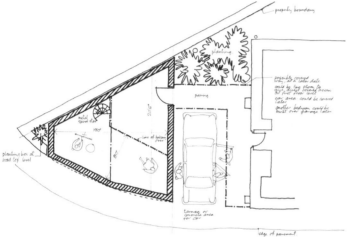

property boundary

planting

possibly covered area, at a later date

could be two storeys to give direct access at first floor level

car area could be covered later

another bedroom could be built over garage later

planting

metal spiral stair

1969

line of balcony over

parking

planting box at street top level

terrace or private area for car

edge of pavement

works. The scheme, which Pearson later described as
"designed for love rather than money", also further
exemplifies Pearson's engagement method in achieving
a wholly positive outcome, something which can be
traced through the recollections of the participants
and the extant written material which, helpfully,
resides with client and architect in separate but
complementary bundles.[33]

Richard Ewen is an artist. Formerly a creative
and art director in the advertising industry, he moved
from the United States to England in 1963 to pursue
landscape, portraiture and still life painting. In 1969
he and his English wife Andi bought a house in the
Wiltshire village of Biddestone, near Chippenham,
although it lacked a studio for Ewen to work in; a
detached garage did come with the house, but this
was neither heated nor day-lit. Funding some form
of extension, however, would be difficult for the couple
as Ewen sought to establish his new career.

As with Mayford, Pearson's involvement in
the Ewens' dilemma began unusually; in Pearson's
words, Ewen:

met my father-in-law in a pub and exchanged
a picture for ready cash [He and Andi] got
together [...] They bought their new house and
I created a studio.[34]

That brief description disguises three years of close
liaison with the Ewens over the project, beginning
with a brief which called for a work space large enough
to accommodate Ewen's canvasses, quiet enough to
allow productive labour yet close enough to the house
for an easy transition from the pleasure of dinner
parties to the business of showing work to prospective
clients. And all this in the context of a house from
around the late 18th century situated just off the green
of a picturesque Cotswold village, perhaps the most
challenging location for a contemporary architectural
intervention that could be imagined, and on a very
restricted budget. As Pearson recalls, "It had to be dirt
cheap, cheap as possible."[35]

Using the wedge-shaped garage site which had
a good aspect to the north, Pearson's initial idea was
for a free-standing two-storey studio with a split
double-pitched roof to give the north light that has
been desired by artists for generations. An open-air
parking space provided separation from the house,
minimising visual conflict between the two structures.
Phased expansion to suit the available budget
envisaged the studio and house joined by a simple
covered way initially and later a two-storey, built link,
whilst the parking space could first be enclosed and
then have a bedroom added above it in due course.
Such consideration would come to the fore much later
in Pearson's vast hospital projects. Landscaping of the
site — modest, but completely in keeping with Pearson's
previous work — completed this scheme.

When Pearson sent this plan to Richard Ewen
in July 1969, he did so with a disarmingly-phrased
exhortation which perfectly encapsulates his self-
critical style and his views on client involvement:

I would like you to criticise these proposals as severely as you can so that we can find out whether they fail to meet your requirements.[36]

Pearson did indeed rework the scheme thereafter, evolving the design further and proving the power of the iterative process which he has made his own.

Reviewing an idea present in the earlier design, Pearson determined that, rather in the manner of a commercial air rights development, the studio could in fact be located in the 'free' space over the existing garage. This would increase the amount of north light available, simplify the window arrangement, allow the studio to be permanently — and thus more conveniently — joined to the house from the outset and free more of the available plot for other uses. The revised scheme thus essentially inverted the previous proposal.

Pearson decided to rebuild the existing garage though on the same footprint, at an angle to the house; the differing orientations avoided a monolithic silhouette and reflected the relaxed placement of village buildings. The simpler roofline was more in keeping too.

To connect the studio to the house Pearson designed a two-storey structure with great attention to detail. Generously glazed and narrowed at its upper level to reduce bulk and emphasise the difference between the new and the old, it provided direct access to the studio both from the master bedroom and the street, via a new front door and a spiral stair.

Masterfully, the stair was placed near but not opposite the existing kitchen door, fully linking both structures but reserving the position on axis with that door for an artificially top-lit niche to hold one of the Ewens' Italian statues. A subtle detail, this demonstrates just how closely the work was tailored to its owners, as this was also aimed at creating an impressive entry for potential clients.

As letters show, adjustments followed over the following months to hone both men's visions, mostly concentrating on internal arrangements. A mutually supportive engagement is clear. In January 1970, for example, Andi Ewen wrote to Pearson saying "We have heard nothing but praise from everyone for your designs."[37] For Richard Ewen, as client and end user of the studio, maintaining his vision during this process was important:

At one stage I was a little bit nervous about what was going to happen, and then I thought, it'll all come right as long as I'm all right. And once I'd decided that this was all going to work in my head, then it has.[38]

Of course planners' objections to such ideas as the space between the rear of the garage and the rear of the house being used as a bedroom were also addressed as part of this; Pearson altered the space to a storage and laundry area.

In February Pearson sent the Ewens a model of the scheme as it currently stood to aid their understanding of how the spaces would be organised. The impact of this is striking. Richard Ewen wrote

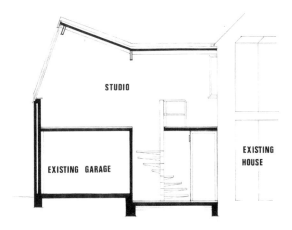

afterwards that "I have sat for hours just looking at your marvellous model and can visualise very well painting better pictures", whilst today Andi Ewen remembers with delight how "Michael [...] sent us this big box and out of this box came the studio."[39]

Pearson introduced the same adaptability for the end user allied with thoughtful service provision as in his much larger projects. Natural light from the north light could be adjusted by roller blinds and either supplemented by artificial light in varying amounts from dimmer-controlled, moveable spotlights mounted on tracks or completely replaced by fluorescent light from tubes at the head of individual panes. Flaps below the same panes gave ventilation.

Remarkably, despite the highly bespoke nature of the job, Pearson allowed for the possibility of a future change of owner by demonstrating how the studio could be converted to bedrooms. The significance of this in light of later works will become clear.

When it came to the exterior finish for the new structures, difficulties were perhaps inevitable given the location. The planning authority demanded natural stone but this would have been prohibitively expensive, although the Ewens did locate a supplier of reclaimed stone. Pearson accordingly argued against this, relying on his knowledge and previous experience for an ingenious alternative:

I had learnt quite a lot of lessons when I went on the concrete block tour of the States. By that time Forticrete had got a plant going [in Britain] where they were making these two-inch blocks and then cutting them, so you got a rock face; they were just done in a brake press with a great big knife like that and banged on each side.[40]

Forticrete had also supplied the American-originated blockwork for Shackcliffe school, a first at that time, and so Pearson worked with the firm to produce a

concrete block which could closely match the buff Cotswold stone used in Biddestone. For the colour,

we got them to come down here and they used a special sand to make the block [...] They did a whole run and they sold the rest to somebody else [...] They came over here and had a look at the existing [buildings to help select] both the coarse aggregate and the fine sand – it was a fine [...] light brown sand.[41]

For texture, the blocks "were made twice the width [of the standard 2"/50.8mm block] and split in the middle" so that the rough, split sides of the halved 16 x 4" (406mm x 102mm) block could face outwards to form the exterior walls.[42] The same split-faced block lined the interior of the spiral stairwell and the statue niche, contributing to the luxurious feel of the entry area.

With the form of the studio finally agreed, construction began in July 1970. Felix J Samuley and Partners again provided the engineering. Throughout, the exchange between client and architect continued to drive the project, often amusingly. "I'll try not to think of another thing!"[43] apologised Andi Ewen in August, though by September Pearson's site representative was being questioned regarding a picture rail, storage frame for canvases and hessian wall lining. Andi Ewen was also keen to be involved in the interior design, which Pearson encouraged. Principal construction took until December that year to complete although additional work, including fabrication and installation of the purpose-designed spiral stair in tubular steel, occurred over the two following summers.

Had Pearson built a contemporary addition to a traditional vernacular building and setting without unduly compromising either? When the studio was published, articles made clear its newness but praised its suitability for the site. For Building Design, "Extending village life needn't mean slipping into the vernacular", whilst Building called the studio

"modern yet unobtrusive", "one of those all-too-rare cases in which an extension has been very successfully integrated into the village without resorting to pastiche".[44] Not entirely unexpectedly, Concrete Quarterly approved, declaring that "the studio undeniably belongs to this age, but more importantly it appears to be firmly rooted in its village. And yet it employs 'modern' materials."[45]

Today, the Ewen studio fits beautifully in its environment, a village often claimed to be the prettiest in England. It is a piece of modern architecture, certainly, but the calm, undemonstrative form it adopts allows it to be appreciated as such without jarring. The passage of nearly forty years has mellowed the split concrete blockwork which blends even more sympathetically with the quartz-flecked stone of the house, a painstaking variation on Pearson's contextual usage of materials. Inside, the compact, efficient, elegant plan impresses. The quality of workmanship is superb.

But what really strikes one is the sheer pleasure the building gives its occupiers, surely the ultimate proof of architecture's worth and, for Pearson, the power of process. For Andi Ewen, "it's magic, absolutely magic [...] the whole thing has been perfect".[46] For Richard Ewen, whose very personal needs drove this project, its importance is clear:

I love coming up here... coming here in the morning [...] It's a lovely arrangement because it's tucked away so nicely and there's no bother with sound or anything.[47]

Indeed, after recent serious illness, Pearson's work has been fundamental in Richard Ewen's recovery:

It is extraordinary... the other day I was sitting here and I really didn't know where I was going from here. Everything had closed down now. So I didn't know what I was going to do, how to go about it, and I was ill, so I had to make a decision, and the decision I made was, just stay in this room and paint – it'll all come right. And that's pretty much how it's working.[48]

The Ewen studio is a Pearson miniature; the smallest of his many projects, yet still containing each element of the Pearson philosophy. It was designed entirely on a "human scale", simultaneously with the mammoth project that was Burne House.[49] As to the matter of the material used, Pearson likes to relate how "A planning officer telephoned after it was completed to congratulate me on its harmony with the village and how much he admired the natural stone work."[50]

The final comment, though, should perhaps belong to Richard Ewen: "I adore it."[51]

The final pair of projects examined in this chapter actually predate the Ewen studio and the Turton school pool conceptually (neither was realised) but it is only by isolating and examining them at this stage that the path from Pearson's earlier works to Burne House, covered in the following chapter, becomes clear because of their direct impact on that building.

Pearson's most radical designs yet, they once again – though arguably to the greatest extent to date – brought together provision for change, differentiated servant and served space and responsiveness to the building's surroundings, generated by a process of methodical revision.

Between 1965 and early 1966, Charles B Pearson Son & Partners were commissioned by the Ministry of Public Building and Works to design the Lancaster Crown Local Office, which was to bring together in one building various central government services that were provided at a local level.

Initial discussions with the client showed that the most important criteria were that all accommodation should ideally be on the same level, staff with the most contact with the public had in any event to be situated on the ground floor and, given the nature of central government, the proposed building be as flexible in use as possible to accommodate frequent departmental reorganisation. A quality working environment was also required, but within a limited budget.

As at Mayford, an expectation of a conventional solution existed but Pearson thought it restrictive and unresponsive to the brief:

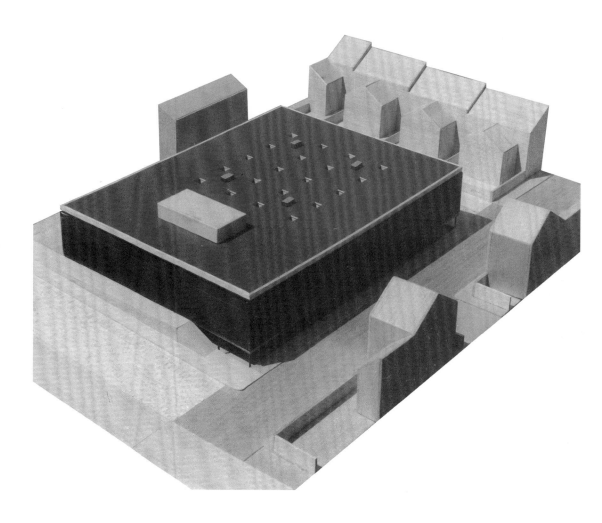

Above and opposite top
Model photographs depict interior and exterior of the Lancaster Crown Local Office.

Opposite bottom
Maximum packing study.

When Lancaster started it was [a] standard office block, and then if you wanted a big room you missed a couple of partitions out, that was all there was to it.[52]

This standard block would have had narrow floorplates for daylight but this would have made internal change difficult and been incompatible with the demand for accommodation across a single floor – which itself was incompatible with the ability of such a typical block to provide natural light to all users.

Pearson thus conjectured how the Lancaster site might be used more efficiently. Based on volumetric analysis, he:

did a maximum packing study showing that this site will accommodate that amount of accommodation. And I think you'll find that if you take all those upper floors and put them together, the volume is the same. Once you got the maximum volume through that you were able to do it in different ways.[53]

That the site could in fact take a lower, wider building that would provide the same area as a higher block of much narrower floors was a decisive early conclusion. Pearson recalls the next step:

And I remember drawings that were L-shaped, and then we started to try and get – because it's a sloping site – parking at lower level. And then I remember quite clearly we decided to put the other side of the L around here and miss that [space between them] out.[54]

In arriving at this solution, Pearson had crystallised a line of thinking he had been following since 1963, around "a system of space organisation and construction" for offices that would ease "changing the planning and improving the internal environmental conditions within the normal low budget cost".[55] He had become absorbed by the apparent possibilities of low, deep-plan structures, and this was the turning point.

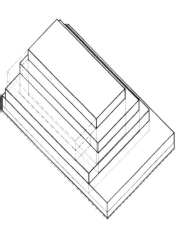

The result was a single-storey, high-ceilinged, steel-framed building with over 60 per cent of its 22,630 square feet (2,100 square metres) of accommodation on the ground floor and the remainder on a mezzanine or gallery level suitable for those functions requiring privacy or security.

As well as Pearson's own interest in adaptability, major influences on his designs for Lancaster were Neville Cooley's offices for the West Midlands Gas Board, Solihull, 1961–1962, a single large principal volume with air conditioning and daylight through the roof, in England; Ehrenkrantz's SCSD system and Skidmore Owings & Merrill's Connecticut General Insurance Company, Connecticut, 1954–1957, a vast, column-free workspace, in the United States; and Walter Henn's administration building for OSRAM in Munich, 1963–1965, of relatively standard multi-storey curtain-walled construction but, internally, one of the earliest examples of *bürolandschaft* in Germany, which Pearson had visited.[56] The Solihull building, especially, had considerable parallels

with Lancaster, having been originally intended as a seventeen-storey block, a sloping site and a requirement for high-quality interiors.

To ensure adequate daylight in such a deep plan, windows supplying principally the cellular gallery rooms were supplemented by rooflights for the main open office area. In a telling recollection of his earlier work at Lancaster Royal Grammar School, Pearson gave the best view – of Morecambe Bay to the west, and this only from above ground level – to the canteen positioned on the gallery.

Then as now, office buildings were planned to grids. As Pearson explains,

> We were all tied up with modular co-ordination
> [...] so you know where to locate things so they
> connect automatically... I liked grids, still do.[57]

At Lancaster, the structural module was 4' (1.2m) giving wide column spacings of 16' (4.9m). The linked planning module was 2' (0.6m) allowing for cellular rooms of any multiple of this size.

Importantly, extendibility was also possible simply by adding additional structural bays as needed with further service cores added "at critical points".[58] A Kahnian view of the building's services, vital to support the notion of a changeable interior, informed their arrangement: "Fixed elements; the stairs, lavatories, flues and vertical services are tightly clustered together to give the minimum intrusion into the total available space".[59] For heating and cooling the open area, conventional convector heaters were insufficient,

> because you can't do this kind of thing without blown air, you can't do it with pipes and radiators which are part convection and part radiation [because] the hot air goes up to the top of the ceiling and the folk in the middle freeze.[60]

During his 1962 research tour of the United States, Pearson had driven between San Francisco and nearby Palo Alto along El Camino Real, the route connecting the missions built when California was under Spanish rule. Now a modern freeway, it comprised in part a "high street 50 miles long" lined with simple concrete block shops and offices.[61] However, Pearson saw that

> They had air conditioning through the roof. And of course I saw it in all sorts of other places. They had the air conditioning units that we didn't have – Lennox air conditioning [...] I rang Lennox in the States to see whether they would be able to supply them if we got this job and they sent all sorts of useful information. They were making some kinds of fans in this country but not really the sort of thing that we were looking for. These were air conditioning units on which you put trunking and had an outlet and you could move these things around because the trunking was flexible, that was the idea [...] You've got no pipes around the perimeter [with this type of unit].[62]

Lennox later won a contract to supply the SCSD programme and their air conditioning was a major element in its success. Following Cooley at Solihull, believed to be the first to adopt the concept in Britain, Pearson thus mounted self-contained, packaged air conditioners on the roof at Lancaster, which could then feed via the minimum run of ducting necessary to outlets in the ceiling directly below.[63]

In this way the services were not only grouped in servant spaces but had an ability to change, reflecting the adaptability of the space they served. To take just one example of how this change was envisaged, space for car parking, enabled by the slope of the land, could be exchanged for additional plant, or indeed storage.

The final element in the building's capacity for change was its skin, and here Pearson took the next step along a line of highly original thought which had begun with Joseph Paxton and the Crystal Palace, London in 1851, where a structural frame was closed with non-load-bearing, same-sized panels of solid boarding, glazing or doors, and continued through Godfrey Greene's Sheerness Boat Store, Kent of 1860, now regarded as the world's first multi-storey building with a rigid metal frame whose exterior walls, serving no structural purpose, are merely lightweight galvanised corrugated iron infill panels.

For the Lancaster Crown Local Office, Pearson designed the exterior so that it could accept "solid panels or fixed and opening lights in any desirable arrangement" following the planning module.[64] Thus public access doors were able to be relocated anywhere along two sides of the building.

This was a key intellectual leap in the architecture of surfaces, a fully interchangeable cladding system for the exterior that could be altered at any time after completion to reflect changes to the interior (neither Paxton's nor Greene's panels were designed to be changed once installed). The idea was developed in

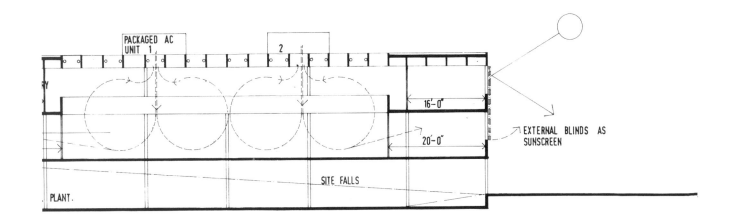

PACKAGED AC UNIT 1

2

16'-0"

20'-0"

EXTERNAL BLINDS AS SUNSCREEN

SITE FALLS

PLANT.

RY

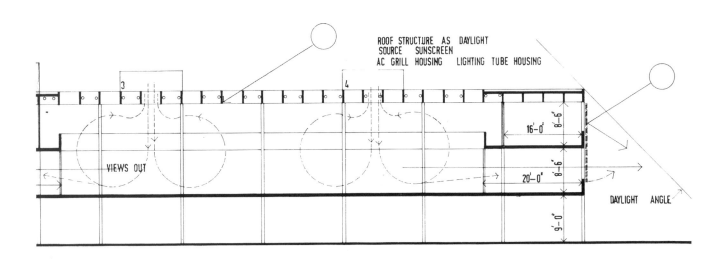

ROOF STRUCTURE AS DAYLIGHT SOURCE SUNSCREEN

AC GRILL HOUSING   LIGHTING TUBE HOUSING

3

4

16'-0"

20'-0"

8'-6"

8'-6"

9'-0"

VIEWS OUT

DAYLIGHT ANGLE

0   25   30 FEET SCALE

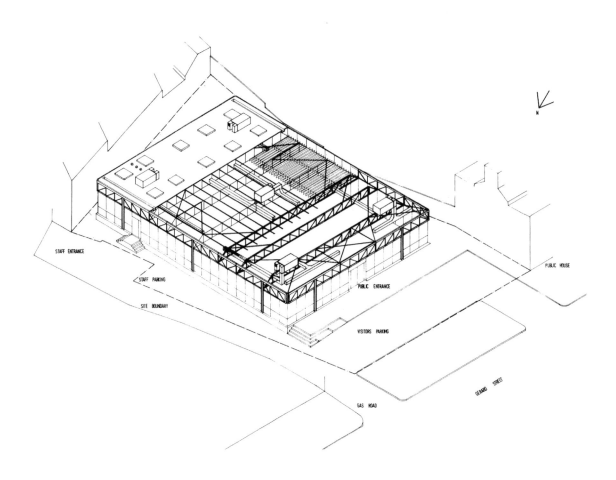

STAFF ENTRANCE
STAFF PARKING
SITE BOUNDARY
PUBLIC ENTRANCE
VISITORS PARKING
PUBLIC HOUSE
GERARD STREET
GAS ROAD

This superb axonometric illustrates the principal features of the winning Ashton Crown Local Office design, particularly the layers of the roof construction including the packaged air conditioners and their trunking.

Pearson's unexecuted design for a second Crown Local Office, discussed below, and opened the way to Burne House as built pioneer, as will be seen.

Unfortunately changes of client direction caused the abandonment of the Lancaster scheme which therefore remained unbuilt. However, close examination of Pearson's responses to this commission show that he not only satisfied the brief – and as at the Ewen studio and other earlier works, a sense of economy was also present – but espoused theories and practices which would have a profound effect on both his own work and that of others. His building could be remodelled almost entirely, including a change in orientation with respect to the street and even an unlimited expansion of its footprint, for a range of current and future users, and in this, too, Burne House had its roots.

The unsatisfactory end to this commission did not deter Pearson from entering a Ministry competition, later in 1966, to design other Crown Local Offices for various sites in Britain. The competition brief contained a number of specific requirements,

the most prominent of which were a building "capable of change", as Pearson put it later, and with the maximum amount of space within its envelope.[65] For Pearson, the peculiarities of the competition entry rules were providential:

If you were in the north west, Ashton [-in-Makerfield, Greater Manchester] was the site; if you were in the north east, some [where] else, but if you were in London, you could choose – privilege for the Londoners. So what we had a look at was [...] every one of the sites and found which one would take the accommodation in a single storey building, and it was only Ashton [that would enable us to] design a deep plan; there was more flexibility or more adaptability in a deep plan.[66]

Pearson's entry for the Ashton Crown Local Office competition adopted principles present in the Lancaster scheme, but broadened and developed them in many ways.

Calculating the widest possible building able to be fitted on the site (64'/19.5m), Pearson worked with Arup to create the structure. Adopting the same modular approach as at Lancaster for simplicity and cheapness, a standard unit emerged comprising a 9' (2.7m) column supporting a Howe truss 4' (1.2m) deep and cantilevered 12' (3.7m) each side of the column. The resulting T-shaped units were to be linked by 8' (2.4m) or 16' (4.8m) sections of Howe truss referred to as connecting ties – "What we did was we had a T there and a T there connected by an intermediate piece which gave it its stability."[67]

Although SCSD was influential, and Charles B Pearson Son & Partners was, along with other British firms such as RMJM, using various constructional systems at this time including CLASP, not least at Turton school's main buildings, Pearson was also informed by his admiration of the works of French metal worker and designer Jean Prouvé.[68]

Venerated on the continent, Prouvé was born the same year as Kahn to an artist father and was apprenticed to a blacksmith and then a metal workshop. He rapidly became an accomplished furniture designer but in parallel also began to explore the application of metal to architecture. Beginning with ornamental worked iron – grilles, handrails, balconies – and then more practical items such as moveable partitions and lift cages, Prouvé moved on to design a wide range of pre-fabricated buildings with structural and architectural components: pavilions such as the Aero Club Roland Garros (1936), easily-transportable emergency housing for wartime refugees, barrack units and schools. This progression climaxed after World War II with entire facade systems featuring complex layers of materials and mechanisms.

Prouvé's output married the traditional skills of working materials and manipulation that he had learned in his youth to new concepts of how metal could be used, always emphasising its lightness,

strength and temperature-controlling properties and striving for aesthetically acceptable as well as technically functional results.

Prouvé was to be directly involved in the development of Burne House's cladding, but it was Pearson's exposure, whilst a student, to Prouvé's early designs which assisted the Ashton Crown Local Office.

Appreciating the economy and elegance of the joints in Prouvé's furniture, which often used bolted elements, Pearson also noted Prouvé's ability to design structures for both his furniture and his buildings which were conceptually identical and differed only in scale. Exploring an exhibition devoted to Prouvé during preparation of the present work, Pearson noted examples of this:

These elbow joints – they're there, in that [table] leg shape, which is the point of weakness which is stiffened, rather like [the building] over here [...] Here's the building-sized frame, here's the desk-sized frame.[69]

Pearson took Prouvé's 'stiffened elbow' or portal frame and applied it to the main structure of the Ashton Crown Local Office. Thus two standard units linked by a 16' connecting tie were sufficient to span the 64' width of the site, whilst repeating the module of standard unit plus 8' connecting tie along the length of the site gave the outline structural framework.

Improving on Lancaster, the Ashton building's roof was formed from transverse trusses, 64' long as determined by the plot width, with diagonal wind braces, giving a column-free interior. With a site length of 88' (26.8m) this yielded a single-storey building with an area of over 5,500 square feet (500 square metres) which could be occupied and divided as needed.

Pearson now turned to the servicing of the building. As at Lancaster the only fixed services were the lavatories and water supply but in an improvement of the earlier scheme they were pushed

Opposite

Section showing partition
heights, suspended ceiling and
air conditioning arrangement
within ceiling.

to the very edge of the building envelope where they
would least affect space planning. Air conditioning
was again mounted on the roof, five 3-ton/tonne units
having their trunking contained within the depth of
the roof trusses. Ingeniously, electrical and telephone
cabling passed through inflated tubes cast into the
poured concrete floor slab along the north and south
walls and transversally at 8' (2.4m) centres giving
outlets every 24' (7.3m).

For the skin of the building Pearson used thin
(2"/5cm), 'sandwich' or laminated panels of foam
cement, aluminium foil and cement asbestos to provide
insulation and fire protection, something Finnish
architect Eero Saarinen had introduced between 1948
and 1956 at his General Motors Technical Center at
Warren, Michigan. Saarinen's panels were finished
externally with an enamel coating, something Pearson
was to use at Burne House, but at Ashton the panels
were to be faced with Eternit, a proprietary material
composed of fibrous cement and here subject
to the emaille process whereby colour is fixed at
manufacture by thermal and chemical bonding.

As at Lancaster, these panels shared the same
modular sizing as the doors which could again be
placed in any position, this time along the west facade.
Rooflights were now the principal means of supplying
natural light, giving an even distribution throughout
and reducing heat loss and solar gain; windows were
few due to the perceived poor views available but
where used also followed the module and were sealed
with gaskets of neoprene, a synthetic rubber.

Neoprene as an architectural component had only
come to Britain as recently as 1966 with the completion
of the Cummins Engine Factory at Darlington, County
Durham by Roche and Dinkeloo, successors to Saarinen
after his death; Saarinen had also originated the idea at
Warren after seeing its use in the fitting of car glazing,
although Prouvé is credited with developing it by
inventing a compressible neoprene gasket.

Pearson's early use of a new material again marks
out the Crown Local Offices as a point of change in
his work, particularly when compared to his broadly
traditional approach to date. This borrowing of
repeatable, machine-made, dry-fit components from
other industries was also practised by Prouvé, who
looked particularly to aeronautical companies and their
experience with metals as both structure and skin. Here
again Pearson followed Prouvé's lead for Ashton:

> We were in touch with all sorts of manufacturers
> of aircraft components. We got in touch with
> some firm who made the floors; I mean, two
> skins of aluminium, incredibly stiff, they had a
> kind of eggshell form inside, which made them
> very good load-bearing material.[70]

Collectively, all of the above – the orientation, the
structure, the servicing and the cladding – were
intended to produce one result; to design into the
scheme capacity for change from the outset. To
illustrate this, the final building was depicted space-
planned in various configurations, ranging from a
"minimal enclosure" with no partitioning at all and
suitable for *bürolandschaft* to a conventional fully
cellular office.[71] Pearson's design could accommodate
all of these and more; in seeking to create a regular,
standardised building that could nevertheless adjust
to the irregular activities within it, Pearson was
abiding by a key principle of the International Style
as expounded by Henry-Russell Hitchcock and Philip
Johnson as long ago as 1932.[72]

Pearson's entry into the Ashton competition
won Charles B Pearson Son & Partners first prize,
a resounding vote of confidence in the skill and
innovation he employed for this remarkable scheme
and a very fitting continuation of his father's and
grandfather's legacy. When published in March 1967,
the scheme was described as "a brave attempt [...]
to push the frontier back, in both construction and

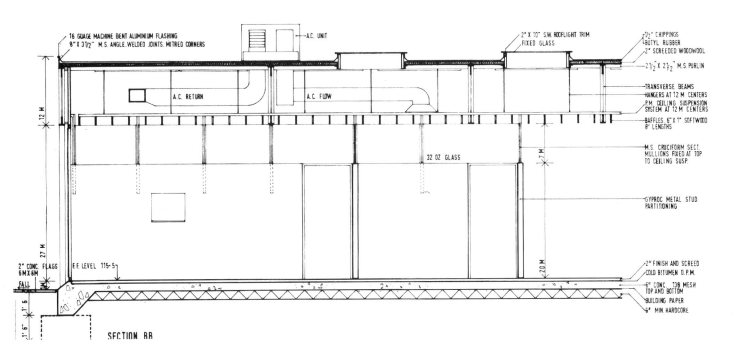

16 GUAGE MACHINE BENT ALUMINIUM FLASHING
8" X 3½" M.S. ANGLE. WELDED JOINTS. MITRED CORNERS

A.C. UNIT

2" X 10" S.W. ROOFLIGHT TRIM
FIXED GLASS

1½" CHIPPINGS
BUTYL RUBBER
2" SCREEDED WOODWOOL

2½" X 2½" M.S. PURLIN

TRANSVERSE BEAMS
HANGERS AT 12 M CENTERS
P.M. CEILING SUSPENSION
SYSTEM AT 12 M CENTERS

BAFFLES. 6" X 1" SOFTWOOD
8' LENGTHS

M.S. CRUCIFORM SECT.
MULLIONS FIXED AT TOP
TO CEILING SUSP.

GYPROC METAL STUD
PARTITIONING

A.C. RETURN

A.C. FLOW

32 OZ GLASS

12 M

.7 M

27 M

.20 M

2" CONC. FLAGS
6 M X 6 M

F.F. LEVEL 115·5

2" FINISH AND SCREED
COLD BITUMEN D.P.M.

6" CONC. 136 MESH
TOP AND BOTTOM
BUILDING PAPER
6" MIN. HARDCORE

FALL

1' 6

1' 6

SECTION BB

environmental design" and "a more forward-looking approach to industrialised building".[73]

Astonishingly, though, the Ashton scheme, too, was to remain on the drawing board after – ironically – government reorganisation resulted in the creation of a new Ministry for Social Security, one of whose earliest actions was to close its office in Ashton. Pearson remembers

> The Minister of Works' letter... paragraph one: congratulations on winning the scheme, herewith enclosed a cheque for the sum of 500 pounds, paragraph two: we're very sorry but it's been cancelled because we've reassessed the need.[74]

Despite this, the two Crown Local Office schemes are pivotal.

They embrace all three of Pearson's definitions of change. Adaptability of the internal area arose from an unencumbered plan as a fully served space, cabling, heating, lighting and ventilation having been provided to any point within that space. Extendibility was assured by the structural system, the modular portal frame being able simply to be multiplied to whatever extent was necessary. Flexibility was inherent in the structural frame and concrete foundation slab, which could between them accommodate settlement and additional loading such as alternative air conditioner units or heavier cement block partitions. Future users, perhaps very different from those who first occupied the buildings, were also catered for from the outset, making provision for change truly far reaching.

The process, too, proved vital, examination and re-examination of the brief and the available tools leading to the desired outcome. This also confirms Pearson's indifference toward 'style' and preference for the methods and materials that satisfy the needs of a given job, always refracted through the needs of client and user. Thus Kahnian influences continued but Pearson was clear that – as he puts it – having the structure of a building determine where you put your deckchairs is too definitive an application of a given doctrine.

The Crown Local Offices are wholly modern and innovative designs that gathered technology and techniques from a rich range of sources to create light (bright + weight), changeable envelopes of effective, economic working space. The pared-down, functional, efficient Modernist 'shed', whether clad in brick or glass or other material, was always deemed acceptable for factories; Pearson moved this acceptability to the office.

The buildings remind one inescapably of the future work of Norman Foster, Richard Rogers and Nicholas Grimshaw, who came to favour the impermanence and potential for change offered by steel framing and lightweight cladding and whose crossover and merging of aesthetics and components from other design fields (refrigerated truck panels and bus windows were used by Rogers for his houses from 1968, caravan technology by Foster for his Renault Centre at Swindon in 1982, yacht rigging by Grimshaw at the British pavilion for the 1992 Seville Expo) would prove critical to defining the High Tech movement.

Foster, for example, built a very similar single-storey, steel-framed box for IBM at Cosham, Hampshire, in 1970-1971, although this was fully glazed. The Ashton design also comes very close to Rogers' concept of a building as a simple "container" for functions rather than an architectonic volume per se, although the word was used by Rogers a decade later to describe his winning entry in the 1971 Pompidou Centre competition.[75]

Pearson anticipated all of this by some years, and though he would not enjoy being described as a High Tech architect, it seems entirely appropriate to use Rogers' words to summarise a less well known forerunner of the ideas that would be set out in Paris, through a competition which Pearson would also enter – and yet this was for Pearson simply a development of his previous work in this area.

The Crown Local Offices were ahead of their time and their legacy is all around. Forty years on, a British firm currently offers a modular building system whose centrepiece is a pre-fabricated, five metre square "roof cassette" that contains all necessary services as well as optional rooflights and is simply mounted on columns with walls and partitions added – additional units are connected together as needed.[76] The names of Foster, Rogers and Grimshaw – all contemporaries of Pearson, having been born in 1935, 1933 and 1939 respectively – will recur in the current narrative owing, it will be proposed, a considerable debt to him even beyond the Crown Local Offices.

Pearson's view of the projects is succinct:
It would have made our day if any one of those had been built, because they were a straightforward breakthrough; the schools we'd been looking at are just manipulations of knowledge of the time, really, but this, I think did make a breakthrough[77] [...] it would have been a different world.[78]

With these discomfiting episodes in mind and the experience at the AA still fresh, it is unsurprising that, by mid-1967, the United States appeared so attractive.

On his return Pearson settled back into life in an economically sluggish Britain, but believed as he did so that such a climate could in fact be positive for architecture, since
often there is more serious work done in a period of restraint, like the period just after the war [...] it could be a very fruitful and interesting period.[79]

Pearson would not have to wait for very long. After about a year, he was planning a holiday with a friend when he had to cancel; by the kind of fortuitousness that he was becoming familiar with and which often begins great enterprises, the job which was to become Burne House had arrived.

1–21   MP, in conversation with the author, 29 February 2008.

22   MP, email to the author, 19 September 2007.

23   MP, in conversation with the author, 29 February 2008.

24   MP, A note on our attitude to design, Pearson promotional text, 9 May 1977.

25   MP, email to the author, 19 September 2007.

26   MP, in conversation with the author, 29 February 2008.

27   MP, email to the author, 19 September 2007.

28   MP, in conversation with the author, 29 February 2008.

29   MP, in conversation with the author, 1 March 2008.

30   Given their inherent relevance to the scheme as Imperial standards and for ease of reading, these dimensions have not been converted to metric for this section of the text.

31 & 32   MP, in conversation with the author, 1 March 2008.

33   Michael Pearson Associates practice brochure, c. 1996.

34   MP, email to the author, 7 October 2007.

35   MP, in conversation with the author, 27 March 2008.

36   MP, letter to Richard Ewen, 3 July 1969.

37   Andi Ewen, letter to MP, 21 January 1970; Richard Ewen, in conversation with the author, 27 March 2008.

38   Richard Ewen, letter to MP, 10 February 1970; Andi Ewen, in conversation with the author, 27 March 2008.

39–41   MP, in conversation with the author, 27 March 2008.

42   Andi Ewen, letter to MP, 2 August 1970; "Village Fare", *Building Design*, 6 April 1973; "Briefing", *Building*, 30 March 1973; "An artful extension, Briefing", *Building*; "Costwold studio", *Concrete Quarterly*, April–June 1973.

43   Andi Ewen, in conversation with the author, 27 March 2008.

44   Richard Ewen, in conversation with the author, 27 March 2008.

45   Richard Ewen, in conversation with the author, 27 March 2008.

46   MP, "A note on our attitude to design", Pearson promotional text, 9 May 1977.

47   MP, email to the author, 2 January 2008.

48   Richard Ewen, in conversation with the author, 27 March 2008.

49–51   MP, in conversation with the author, 1 March 2008.

52   Charles Michael Pearson, curriculum vitae, c. 1973.

53   At West Midlands, light was adjusted automatically by sensors driving mechanical louvres. "When I was there it was too sensitive so it closed every time a cloud passed, with a great clattering of motors. They later added a 20 minutes time delay" (MP, email to the author, 26 August 2008); OSRAM had desks laid out in the delightful free-form, irregular pattern originally intended by the Hamburg-based Quickborner team who invented it. The rigid, rectilinear desk deployment schemes of many British and American firms both then and now are a dilution of this, although this grid system was also driven by the then-new technology of telephone and electrical points buried in floor screeds which are more naturally placed at regular intervals and thus tend to result in the desks following suit.

54   MP, in conversation with the author, 1 March 2008

55   Lancaster CLO Lancaster Crown Local Office for the Ministry of Public Building and Works, brochure, Charles B Pearson Son & Partners, 1966.

56   Lancaster CLO Lancaster Crown Local Office for the Ministry of Public Building and Works, brochure, Charles B Pearson Son & Partners, 1966..

57–59   MP, in conversation with the author, 1 March 2008; "Open-office Planning, Solihull for the West Midlands Gas Board", *The Builder*, 29 March 1963.

60   Lancaster CLO Lancaster Crown Local Office for the Ministry of Public Building and Works, brochure.

61   Michael Pearson Associates practice brochure, c. 1996.

62   MP, in conversation with the author, 1 March 2008; MP, in conversation with the author, 12 February 2008.

63   One of RMJM's two co-founders was Sir Stirrat Johnson-Marshall; formerly chief architect of the Ministry of Education, he had close involvement with post-war prefabricated building systems for schools.

64   Jean Prouvé—The Poetics of the Technical Object, Design Museum, London, December 2007–March 2008, exhibition organised under the direction of the Vitra Design Museum, Weil am Rhein, in co-operation with the Design Museum Akihabara, Tokyo and the Deutschen Architektur Museum, Frankfurt Main; MP, in conversation with the author, 12 February 2008.

65   MP, in conversation with the author, 12 February 2008.

66   Ashton CLO Ministry of Public Building & Works competition first prize winning design by Charles B Pearson Son & Partners, brochure, Charles B Pearson Son & Partners, undated; Pearson once met Johnson, once again through the efforts of Stirling; he visited his famous glass house at New Canaan, Connecticut, and at the Seagram Building in New York where Johnson had assisted Mies van der Rohe, Johnson demonstrated the strength of the glazing for Pearson by running at it.

67   Alan Diprose, "Forward-looking approach", *The Architects' Journal*, 15 March 1967.

6 Burne House

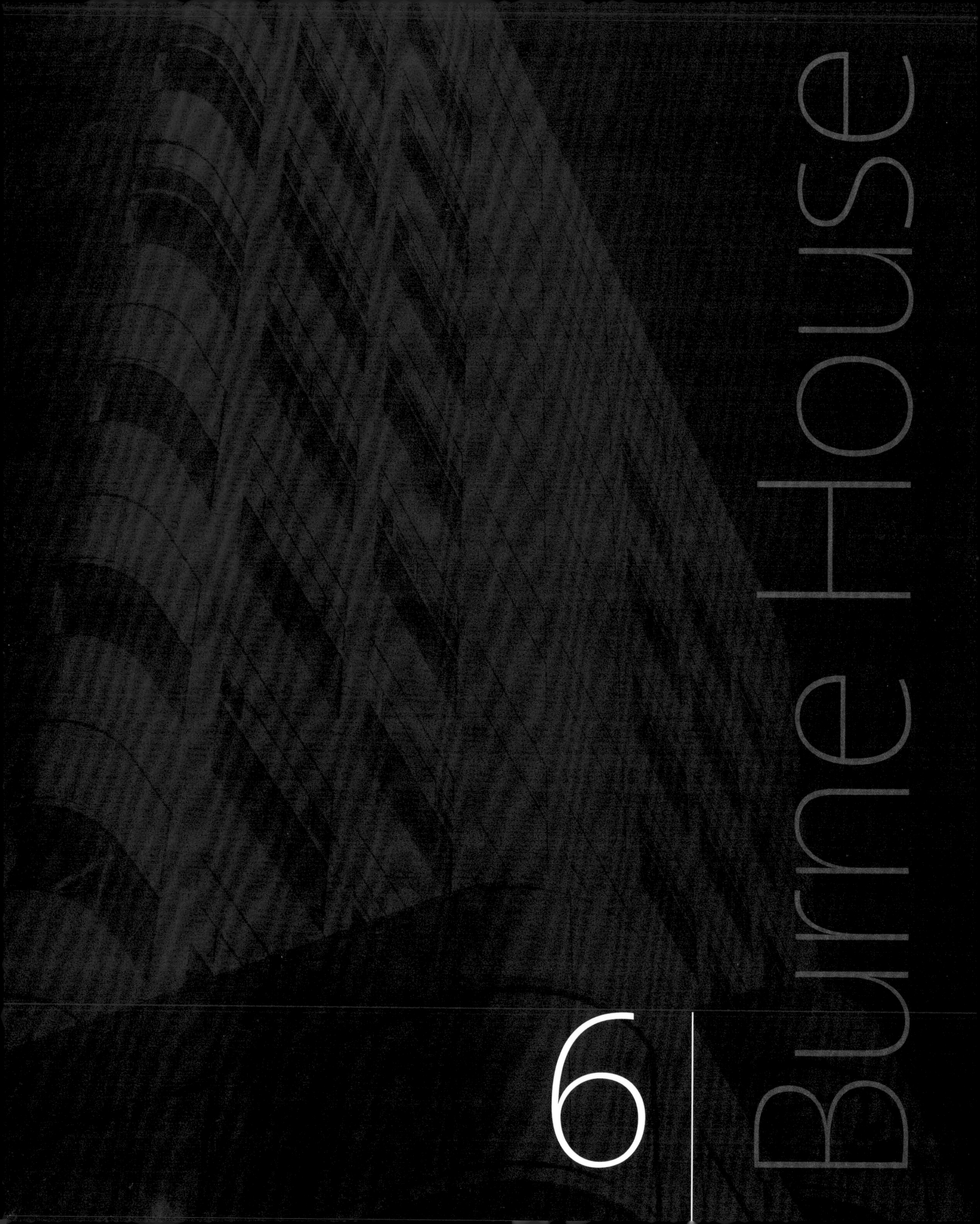

Small massing models showing evolution of the Burne House design through three schemes - cubic tower, two-service-core tower and as built. The extended podium of the first scheme (in darker wood) reflects the full programme originally intended.

The epic Burne House project is the climax of Pearson's built work, bringing together all of his theories, influences and experience to create a building that is unique in its presentation of those theories, influences and experience and original in its use of technology to allow that presentation.

Proven in use, Burne House's adaptable plan, changeable services and innovative, revolutionary cladding system exemplify Pearson's and Roy Landau's concepts of time-based architecture and justify re-examination of other architects' apparently pioneering work in this field, whilst Pearson's success in meeting the extraordinary technical demands of the brief with an aesthetically satisfying building, all within the constraints of a highly prescriptive planning environment, fully prove his practising of a truly inclusive architecture.

Burne House occupied almost ten years of Pearson's life, and he was to return to the building nearly a decade after its completion in a remarkable evaluation of its initial years of operation. The pivot around which his career revolved, Burne House "came out of those earlier schemes and [...] bled into the hospitals" he was to design abroad.[1]

Before considering the building's genesis and design in detail, some appreciation of the client, the site and the protracted coming together of the two is useful.

Client
In the mid-1960s, the Ministry of Public Building and Works began a programme to provide three new buildings across central London for the Post Office in order to meet rapidly increasing customer demand for telephone services.

As with earlier telephone exchanges each would house both staff and apparatus, but even as the Ministry made its plans it was recognised that the nature of that apparatus and the proportion of space allocated to those two very different functions would not stay the same within the new buildings' lifespans.

The technology for routing telephone calls was changing, moving from electro-mechanical Strowger and crossbar switchgear to microprocessor-based electronics.[2] This would not only result in the complete replacement of the equipment initially installed and a significant reduction in its size, but also the automation of operations that would, to begin with, be performed by people.

The pace expected is clear from contemporary estimates that the same operational capability provided by 11 racks of equipment in 1971 would be available from seven racks four years later and just one by 1982; as the Burne House commission was progressing, Duncan McIntyre, deputy controller for the Post Office's London telecommunications region, predicted that by the year 2000 there would be no more telephone exchanges, just manholes.[3]

Yet despite this, the Institution of Post Office Electrical Engineers stated as late as 1967 that "Post Office policy is to plan for at least 100 per cent extension of the initial building which is erected, to cater for the demand up to 20 years after the opening date."[4] The Post Office's assumptions informing their brief for the new buildings were therefore still based on historical precedent at a time when fundamental changes were likely to render such precedent invalid.

It can thus be seen that these new buildings would essentially be the last of their kind. They would be required to accommodate the current generation of apparatus for a number of years yet also be fully compatible with incoming technology, even though the timescale for this was unclear. Major internal alterations would be needed, and services would also have to adapt; electronics require more cooling than mechanical switchgear, and space originally used by equipment might later have to house staff, or vice versa.

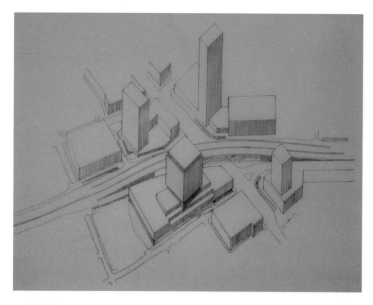

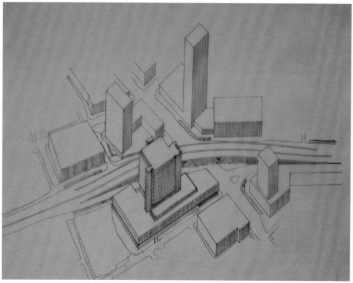

Top
Axonometric, looking south west, of Westminster Council's preferred scheme, retaining the cubic tower. The alignments of the NPTE and the other three buildings in the Council's masterplan are clear.

Bottom
Axonometric of Pearson's first design response, with three fully detached service towers to maximise internal space, in the manner of Kahn.

Opposite
Pearson's second design, with twin, attached service towers, placed within a large model of the site.

It is this requirement for massive change over a building's life, predicted in principle but not in detail from the very start, that was not found in other building types and which was crucial to the design of what was to become Burne House.

Of the programme's three new buildings, later referred to as telecommunications centres in an attempt to reflect the changing environment, one was sited in the City of London (Mondial House on Upper Thames Street) and one in Vauxhall (Keybridge House in South Lambeth Road). The third was destined for Paddington, an area which—entirely co-incidentally—was to provide a remarkable opportunity for client, planner and architect alike.

Site
As the Post Office was formulating its requirements, local government restructuring in London had in 1965 created, inter alia, the borough of Westminster, uniting the former parishes of Westminster, St Marylebone and Paddington. The new borough's authority, Westminster City Council, eager to make its mark and capture the progressive spirit of the times, set out a daring architectural plan for the west of its domain.

In Paddington, 1967 had seen the opening of the Marylebone flyover, the eastern termination of the Westway, an elevated urban motorway which began at White City, ran across London for two and a half miles and now descended, via the flyover, to join Marylebone Road, the two hundred year old east–west road across London. In this, the flyover bridged Edgware Road, the principal north–south route into and out of the city which follows the alignment of the ancient Roman road of Watling Street.

Council planners determined that this uniquely important intersection of ways old and new should be highlighted by a group of four high-rise buildings at the junction of the two roads, placing one on each corner of the crossroads so formed. In a surprisingly

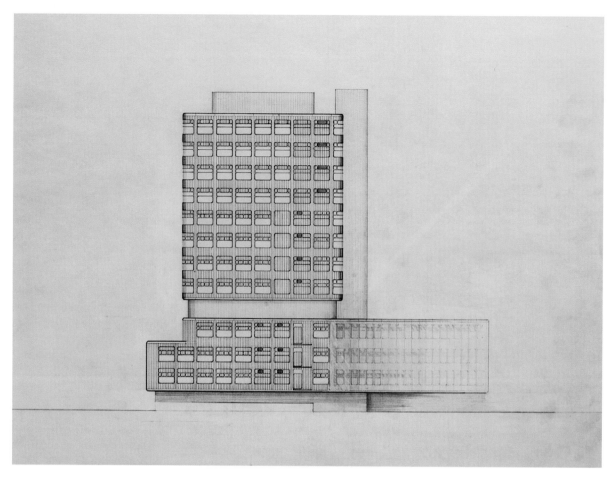

Opposite top
Elevation of the two-core tower scheme, west facade; note the distinctly radiused corners of the cladding panels.

Opposite bottom
Elevation of the final scheme – west facade. Compare with two-core tower iteration.

subtle detail, one diagonally-opposed pair would be orientated parallel to Marylebone Road whilst the other would be aligned with Edgware Road. The resulting composition would form a striking visual gateway to London from the west and north, especially when seen from speeding cars atop the Westway. The Council also hoped that this bold scheme, which also signalled the improved links to the West End facilitated by the Westway and flyover, would sustain the attractiveness of Westminster to companies and organisations seeking to base themselves in London.[5]

Of the four corner plots, that to the southeast had been filled in 1960 with Century House, Richard Seifert's first office tower, and its low, broad podium set the rhythm that the Council wished all four buildings to follow. Thus when the Metropolitan Police took the northwest site for a new divisional police headquarters, careers office and section house (residential accommodation for police officers) the same general pattern was adopted and the complex was aligned north–south with Seifert's, achieved by appropriate placement of the police station's rectangular-plan tower.

Since 1962 the Post Office had been attempting to expand their existing Paddington telephone exchange in Star Street, to the west of Edgware Road, but the then London County Council (LCC), planning authority for the capital, had scheduled the area for housing. In mid-1964 the Post Office approached the outgoing Westminster parish council directly and were offered an alternate site in nearby Irongate Wharf Road, now Harbet Road. The LCC, determiner of the overall form and use of buildings, mandated a tower and podium with shops at street level and flats on some upper floors. Soon afterwards, the Irongate Wharf Road site became the south west corner of the new Westminster City Council's crossroads plan, and so of course the LCC's compositional requirement had to be maintained.

Historically, the Post Office had not considered towers ideal for telephone exchanges—their small floorplates meant services occupied a disproportionate amount of space and made it harder to accommodate personnel rooms immediately adjacent to switchboard rooms, their preferred arrangement. However, noting trends in telecommunications projects abroad, mindful of the delays inherent in obtaining the large sites they required and seeing that towers were becoming popular for hotels, flats and offices, the Post Office was reluctantly changing its mind. In addition, this particular site allowed useful access to vital underground cables serving the area which passed nearby.

Unfortunately, as the Post Office's in-house architect worked to fit its requirements into Irongate Wharf Road, the Council decided that the site should be relinquished in favour of the northeast corner of the new crossroads scheme. The tower and podium would remain, as would mixed use; the Post Office building would now have to incorporate a multi-storey car park, a pub and a rebuilt Edgware Road (Bakerloo Line) London Underground station.

Ironically, the new site was rather too close to the critical cables mentioned above. It was also bisected by a small street and skirted at its northern edge by the Bakerloo Line, but the Post Office accepted it largely because it fulfilled the criteria for expansion outlined earlier. The intention was that the telecommunications centre would ultimately stretch from Edgware Road in the west, across Burne Street, the street separating the two plots, and reach almost to Lisson Street in the east. This would be accomplished in three stages and would lead to the erasure of Burne Street.[6]

The Post Office's decision allowed Seifert to erect a hotel on the Irongate Wharf Road site to complete Westminster Council's quartet of towers and, by confirming the location, provided the final element of the design brief for the Paddington telecommunications centre.[7]

Interestingly no formal name had been chosen for the new building at this stage; initially referred to as Project 10 — Paddington Relief Telephone Exchange, it would be known as the North Paddington Telephone Exchange (NPTE) almost until construction was complete.

Brief

The outline brief for stage one of the NPTE, then, as prepared in late 1967, called for accommodation for switching apparatus to cater for 6,000 simultaneous trunk calls in the area served by the building, plus two local automated exchanges totalling 20,000 lines. Nearly 400 staff would work in the new building, mostly telephonists and operators for calls unable to be routed automatically and directory enquiries. The multi-storey, underground car park comprised a small facility for Post Office personnel with, below it, a much larger public car park to be operated by the Council.

Extraordinary complexity underlay some of the requirements. As well as highly-loaded floorplates and unusually tall floor-to-ceiling heights of 13 feet (3.96 metres), the switching apparatus demanded an array of ancillary services including a freight lift extending 18 floors from the lowest basement to the roof, external loading doors on the podium and four 30-ton emergency backup generators in the basement with tanks containing 24,000 gallons (109,100 litres) of diesel fuel, these needing access from street level and a network of exhaust ducts and radiator shafts. Provision for cabling alone included a 65 yard (60 metre) concrete tunnel, a dedicated lift for cable drums and vertical ducts wider than an average staircase. Stairwells and lift shafts threaded throughout the building, and for security and maintenance reasons the two car parks had to be completely separated from the main building, with their own utility connections, ventilation and access routes.

Despite this list, it would be a mistake to consider the NPTE purely "an industrial building for machinery" as Pearson has modestly described it.[8] The staff complement made the NPTE larger than many standard office blocks, and so the architecture had also to supply spaces for work, training, dining, cooking and relaxation.

The proposed later stages were to expand staffing to around 600, enlarge the public car park and include the pub and Underground station.

In summary the exacting specification for the NPTE, with its integration of elaborate services, large amounts of mechanical plant and significant numbers of personnel, represented an exceptionally specialised building type with few equivalents. The closest contemporary analogue in scale and complexity would be the post-war generation of Fleet Street newspaper buildings, combining as they did press hall and editorial offices on one site. New buildings for The Times (Printing House Square by Llewelyn Davies, Weeks & Partners, executive architects Ellis, Clarke & Gallanaugh, 1960–1965) in Queen Victoria Street and the Daily Mirror (33 Holborn by Owen Williams, 1955–1961) at Holborn Circus were completed as the NPTE was being conceived. These also proved to be the last of their kind for similar technological reasons.[9] Perhaps the only other corresponding building type was represented by the large mail processing complexes of the Post Office itself, such as the West Central District Sorting Office of 1961–1969 by ET Serjent in Bloomsbury, London, with its stacked double-height sorting floors filled with personnel and equipment.

Commission

The Ministry would engage private architects to produce the three new buildings. Hubbard Ford and

The final scheme for Burne House shown on the site model along with the other three towers as built; anti-clockwise, Paddington Green Police station, the Metropole Hotel and Century House.

Partners would design Mondial House and Mills Group Partnership Keybridge House. For Pearson, the opportunity to receive the commission came via a familiarly unconventional route:

> My former wife at the time was working post graduate at the Ministry of Public Building and Works and six [sic] of these buildings were to be erected, so they could not cope. The head of their section had won the competition for Harpenden town hall before the war and beaten father into third place. I was asked to go to see his assistant. They had a plan but no elevation. Could I prepare preliminary working drawings in six weeks? Yes says I.[10]

Only later would the man whose assistant Pearson met come to have a key role in the actual design of the NPTE; for now, for Pearson, fresh from his American experience and the success of the Ashton Crown Local Office competition, the job was a perfect opportunity.

Pearson had no experience of telecommunications structures (which he described later as an advantage) and was aware that, aside from the client's own caveats, a tower was not optimal for any building intended to change throughout its life — the required flexibility is inherently limited by small floorplates piled upon each other.

He had, though, spent several years designing buildings accepting of functional and physical change throughout their lifetime, and had his research and

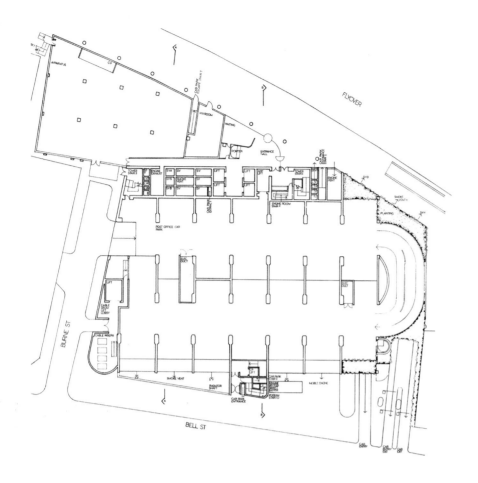

FLYOVER

BURNE ST

BELL ST

Above
Ground floor plan with
parking for vans and access
to Westminster City Council
car park.

Opposite
Third floor of the podium,
with dining and games room
overlooking the flyover.

teaching career in Britain and the United States to call
on. Pearson could also draw a useful parallel between
the new brief and "co-ordinating the complex
engineering services in hospitals", having assisted the
Manchester office by acting as a critic on the Cardiff
competition and given "some input on what I'd learnt
at the Crown Local Offices" to Preston.[11]

Vitally, Pearson had continued to evolve his ideas on
adaptable buildings with Landau following the Crown
Local Offices. Landau had shown a strong interest in
the two projects, which had provided an experimental
platform for testing these ideas in less commonplace
building types, and the pair had subsequently begun to
work together in a very informal fashion, Pearson recalls,
mostly by simply sitting and talking.

This combination of experience and new ideas
was enough to secure the job of producing the
preliminary drawings but, with this task complete,
Pearson's involvement soon deepened.

In September 1968, Pearson anticipated that
full working drawings would be needed early the
following year and suggested taking on an assistant
in readiness; the massive increase in workload that

the job would bring and whether Pearson would
be able to maintain contact with the Manchester
office were discussed by the partnership. In spring
1969 work did indeed start in earnest and would
continue throughout 1969 and 1970 even before a
formal commission to design the NPTE was awarded
to Charles B Pearson Son & Partners, with Michael
Pearson as partner in charge, in December of that year.

Despite that vote of confidence, the challenge
of NPTE was considerable and is caught in a letter
written by Pearson more than three decades later to
Paul Hyett, an active student at the AA when Pearson
was president and later president of the RIBA, in which
Pearson remembers how "my client [...] said, unfolding
some 20 A0 [-sized] drawings, I must comply with
the room layouts of equipment but by the time the
building is completed technology will have changed
his mind or he will be gone and others will have
different objectives".[12]

Concept
Pearson and Landau seized on the core of the NPTE
brief as the perfect demonstrator of stimulus-
response architecture, which requires a degree
of pre-conception of future building uses. Thus
although the precise nature or timescale for new
telecommunications equipment was unpredictable,
the fact of its inevitability was.

This was the key stepping-off point for the
entire NPTE design, finding its purest expression in
the cladding system but also informing the earliest
discussions on the overall form of the new building.

Massing
Pearson had to reconcile the technical demands
of the client with the restrictions imposed by the
Council's masterplan; this included the NPTE having
to be aligned with Marylebone Road and Seifert's
hotel to the southwest. He was also keen to ensure

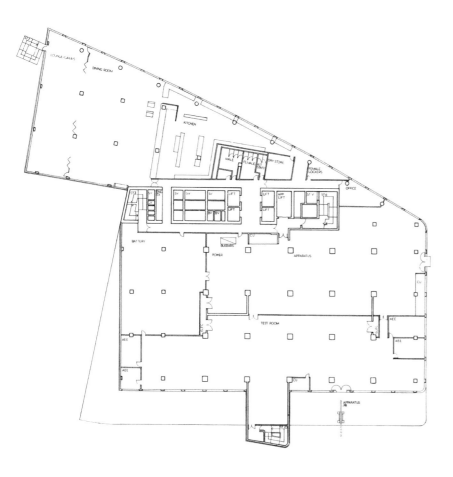

that the new building's visual appearance made a positive contribution to the area; the Post Office itself had called for "an elegant city centre building", and this is what Pearson was determined to provide.[13]

Pearson inherited the planners' wish for the tower to take the specific form of a cube, with rooftop plant projecting above and a floor of reduced area below to create a 'shadow gap' between the tower and the podium. The Post Office disliked the curtailment of usable volume which this produced—for Pearson, the objection was aesthetic: "It was to be a cube sitting on this recessed storey and I fought hammer and tongs against the cube, I thought it was just too gross and too heavy."[14]

Many iterations of tower and podium followed and the small wooden block models which Pearson and the Council pored over make fascinating study.

Pearson's first attempt to persuade the Council and provide his client with as much usable space and flexibility as possible deployed asymmetrically three small detached service towers, each different in plan, around a main tower of regular shape. As Pearson describes,

we were rather worried about this [cubic tower] not providing maximum space and this was just a solution that was provided to Westminster's planner [with] an open floor on every floor and these stair and lift towers external to that space so you got maximum usage out of that space [...]. This was the obvious logical solution.[15]

This scheme is strikingly reminiscent of Richard Rogers' plan for Lloyd's of London, which was not even conceived until 1977, the year Burne House was opened, as well as a second Rogers building 15 years after that, remarkably similar to Pearson's 'three tower' NPTE proposal, explored at the end of this chapter. However, Rogers has explicitly referred to the work of Louis Kahn as influential, and for Kahn, service provision was as important as people provision. He had summed up his approach at the Alfred Newton Richards Medical Research Building in Philadelphia in almost anthropomorphic terms:

My solution was to create three great stacks of studios and attach to them tall service towers which would include animal quarters, mains to carry water, gas and vacuum lines, as well as ducts to breathe in the air from "nostrils" placed low in the building and exhaust it out through stacks high above the roof.... This design, an outcome of the consideration of the unique use of its spaces and how they are served characterises what it is for.[16]

As has been examined, Pearson too was fascinated by Kahn and had by this point seen the Philadelphia building, spent a morning with the architect in his office and already referenced his work at Middleton.

In Pearson's initial design for the NPTE, then, the entire main tower essentially became a 'served space' and Pearson's detached service towers are

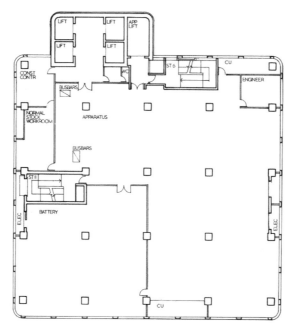

expressions of his affinity for this extreme Kahnian approach where suitable for a client's needs.

Unfortunately it did not prove suitable for Joe Hirsch, the Council's chief planning officer — "He obviously didn't like this because there are too many external shafts [...] He said no, no, it doesn't suit our little balsa wood model to have these projections" — and Pearson was forced to abandon the scheme.[17]

Pearson's next attempt, dating from early 1970, reduced the number of service towers to two by grouping services together and attached them to the main tower as projections from one facade. The underlying cube form was still present. Working drawings were made for this version, indicating the degree of confidence felt by Pearson and his team, but even this was not acceptable, the planning authority insisting "that the circulation was enclosed, more or less, within the envelope".[18]

Pearson was thus finally forced to amalgamate the two service cores into one. This now impinged on the open space within the tower, because one stairwell had as a consequence to be entirely contained within its floor plan. "[The two cores] did get pushed together, that's what he wanted. He would only allow one excrescence externally, but it screws up the availability of space internally because of the escape stair."[19]

In return, though, Hirsch conceded over the cube form, allowing the rooftop plant floor to be enclosed and the recessed storey expanded: "So we got an extra storey and we got this [floor] not being recessed. We got a slightly more elegant tower, being [visually] taller, but there was no compromise on the width."[20]

It should be stressed that no actual height was added to the tower as a result of this deal; careful examination of the massing models confirms that the heights of the towers on all versions are equal. Only the appearance of the ten-storey tower was affected, for the better. Since the tower was square in plan, it was the east–west length of the four-storey podium, particularly

when all three stages had been completed, which was
to fulfil the Council's alignment requirement.

By the autumn of 1970, then, the overall form
had been agreed. The frustration of these negotiations
in the context of a desire to produce a building which
served his client's needs as simply as possible is
reflected in one memory:

> "We also did a sketch of the whole thing
> without a tower, far too late. You know, we
> could get the whole wretched telephone
> exchange in about five storeys just in the
> podium because what they wanted was
> wide open spaces, and a tower was not
> very good [for that]."[21]

Pearson went on to refine the agreed form.

Exterior

The Westway and the Marylebone flyover, designed
by veteran British engineers Maunsell, stood as
emphatic statements of the importance of the
car in the minds of planners of the 1960s. Pearson
understood this, and its implications for the NPTE.
Writing shortly before Burne House's opening,
he outlined his approach:

> This is a large complex building [whose]
> location demands that it is viewed by different
> people in different ways: it is seen in a fleeting
> moment as an elegant tower by motorway
> traffic decelerating on the flyover; it is seen
> at a different scale by slow moving traffic on
> the surrounding streets; at a different scale
> again it is seen at close range by pedestrians
> and particularly by staff entering and leaving
> the building.[22]

Following this principle of differing scales of contact,
Pearson explains how the diagonal width across the
tower concerned him:

> I dreamed about curved corners because I was
> worried about the width of this thing which was
> set in stone. My worry was that I'd looked
> at these little models, and when you look at them
> sideways-on or on the diagonal, it was so bloody
> *wide* compared with its height, and I thought
> well, we'll chamfer them but chamfering didn't
> look right and I just thought, let's put curved
> corners on. I mean just as irrational as that, it
> was just an emotional knee-jerk reaction.[23]

Pearson's route to this solution may have been
unconventional—though a major work by Jean
Prouvé which was to lead to his involvement in
the NPTE design also featured curved corners and
can thus be seen as influential—but the result is
a significant element of Burne House's aesthetic.

Closer to, the scale changes, with the podium
now prominent. To the south its facade gently curves,
following the line of Marylebone Road very closely to
provide a suitable backdrop for the 'decelerating' traffic
on the Westway. In relating at least part of the building
directly to the Westway, Pearson paralleled the work of
another, as by 1968 the Paddington Maintenance Depot
had appeared just a few hundred metres west of the
NPTE site. Designed by Paul Hamilton of Bicknell and
Hamilton to provide office and maintenance facilities
for the vehicle fleet that served British Rail's nearby
Paddington goods yard, its liquid upper storeys form
an almost symbiotic bond with the sweeping lines
of the motorway. Intriguingly, the south facade of the
new police station's podium also seems to have been
tailored for this site—a frieze of large pre-cast concrete
panels appears wholly abstract to those walking next
to it, but from the distance of the road suggests a
parade of figures.

At ground level, in the flyover's shadow, the
scale of the NPTE changes again with a lobby, its
door somewhat hidden and surrounded by smoke

vents. Pearson accepts this is "rather alien" and he "desperately tried to get rid of all those damn smoke ducts" but notes:

> It was never intended to be an entry for staff. It was meant to be an entry for visitors, because they were planning to have tours of schools, groups of interested visitors, who would be taken into this entrance hall. Because the staff all entered from the garage, you know they came in their vans and all of that, or in through that more secure entrance.[24]

Pearson was able to better address the pedestrian's experience at the west end of the podium:

> To soften and humanise this great mass of building a variety of planting has been continued around the ground floor at various levels which will mature and cascade over the perimeter walls. This planting extends into a small garden on the corner of the site where the public will have access to paved areas and seating reminiscent of the many churchyards of the City of London.[25]

The walls of this garden also curved to match the building above, a small reminder of Pearson's subtle concern with how his buildings meet the ground.[26]

Continuing this virtual walk around the planned NPTE, Pearson says he "tried everything" to improve the streetscape in Bell Street, which forms the northern boundary of the site and was, because of its thriving street market, the main pedestrian thoroughfare that the new building would have to respond to: "Over the bridge there's a 30 mile an hour, passing-by contact with the building; Bell Street is walking along with your dog and looking at things in the shop window."[27]

Pearson's suggestion was therefore "to have shops all the way round" the NPTE, complementing the market and ensuring the new building had "contact with the people on the street".[28] It is a sign of Pearson's maturity as much as his philosophy that, in a period when new architecture was often still learning to live with the pre-existing grain of a location, he recognised the reassurance the market provided and sought to supplement rather than destroy it.

Sadly the client did not agree, and vetoed the inclusion of any retail space in the building: "Well, they weren't in the commercial mode in those days; shops, oh we couldn't possibly have shops, security risk, we want total control over our perimeter."[29]

This is of course a fascinating contrast to today's developments in which shops are de rigueur, but Pearson came to accept the situation, realising that "when you find the market, it doesn't matter" and — more wryly — "the market exists even though the building doesn't allow it".[30]

With external design complete, detailed work followed to establish the structural system, layout, services and finish of the building.

Structure and layout

A concrete raft formed the foundations for the basement and tower, with the podium supported by bored concrete piles. The entire site was surrounded by a concrete slurry wall, a relatively new idea which was also being employed at the World Trade Center site in New York throughout 1968 (engineer: Leslie E Robertson). Construction involves digging a short but deep section of trench which is temporarily filled with slurry, a mixture of water and bentonite clay, to prevent collapse and water ingress as it is excavated. When the correct depth has been reached, a steel reinforcement cage is inserted and concrete pumped in; this displaces the slurry. The process is repeated around the site.

The structure above this was a framework of in-situ reinforced concrete columns and floor slabs, the latter cantilevered slightly beyond the perimeter

columns and curved at exterior corners, adhering to Pearson's unconventionally-arrived-at decision; initially planned to be of 6 feet 8 inches (2.03 metres) radius, this was eventually halved to 3 feet 4 inches (1.02 metres) for a more efficient use of space given the apparatus sizes involved. Even here Pearson made allowance for future change, by the unusual device of incorporating 24 x 24 x 12 inch (600 x 600 x 300 millimetres) lightweight concrete blocks into the underside of the poured floor slabs to ease penetration if additional ducting was later required. This also reduced the weight of the slabs whilst creating sufficiently deep and thus strong concrete ribs in both directions to achieve the spans necessary. Two concrete shear walls, continuous from foundation to roof, formed the sides of the tower to give stability.

When disposing the principal constituents of the building, the "Main service and circulation routes [were] grouped and related to main structural elements to give the fixed points in the plan leaving the largest possible free areas of usable space."[31]... as Pearson had done at Middleton and the Crown Local Offices.

The primary passenger lift bank, main stair and freight lift were placed within the single projection from the tower decreed by the planner. The stair that had to be sited within the tower's floorplate as a consequence of that planning decision hugged the external wall to minimise its impact. Pearson's talent for spacial ingenuity and logical arrangement manifested itself in other ways; the freight lift also serves as the fire-

fighting lift for the building, the main stair doubles as a fire refuge and the dry riser is located near to both.

Services

The efficient servicing of the building and especially of its apparatus was imperative, including some capacity to react to the changes that both would be expected to undergo, following the stimulus-response theory.

First, the standard services for any building, albeit here handling a much higher load—power, water and environmental control.

Electrical mains were located in two large ducts adjacent to the shear walls and thus passed uninterrupted through the building vertically. Drawing on his Crown Local Office designs, Pearson located other plant on the roof. A domestic water tank supplied areas aligned directly below on the relevant floors, convectors were sent hot water from boilers and cooling towers and chillers fed cooled water down through grouped pipes to local packaged air handling units on each floor.

It is these units, which draw air through the external 'skin' of the building to be chilled by the water and then fed to the apparatus bays, that are the key to Burne House's inventive cooling system. By separating the more complex step of chilling the water from the simpler step of cooling and circulating the air, Pearson was able to use local air handling units that were smaller than usual and place them with greater freedom. More units could be added if needed and all could be relocated, the final part of the technological jigsaw that allows this being covered in Cladding, below.

This neat, economical and unobtrusive system, also inspired by Pearson's Crown Local Office designs, was a first at the NPTE. As Pearson summarises:

We had packaged air handling units with piped, chilled water—that was all—located near the equipment, *for the first time*. We just happened

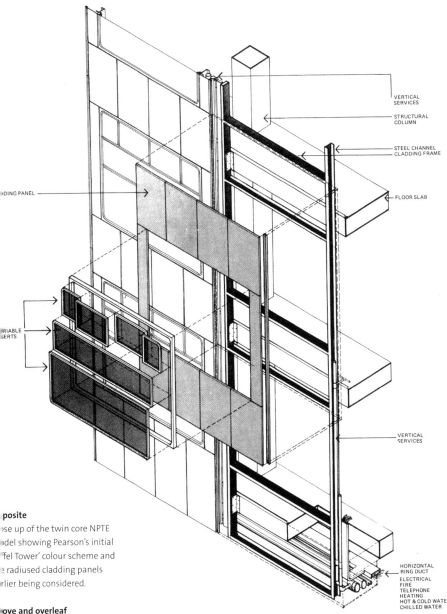

VERTICAL
SERVICES

STRUCTURAL
COLUMN

STEEL CHANNEL
CLADDING FRAME

FLOOR SLAB

...DING PANEL

...RIABLE
...ERTS

VERTICAL
SERVICES

HORIZONTAL
RING DUCT
ELECTRICAL
FIRE
TELEPHONE
HEATING
HOT & COLD WATER
CHILLED WATER

...posite
...se up of the twin core NPTE
...del showing Pearson's initial
...'fel Tower' colour scheme and
...e radiused cladding panels
...rlier being considered.

...ove and overleaf
...metric drawings – based
...original sketches by
...arson – demonstrating the
...ncipal features of the final
...TE cladding system, as seen
...m the exterior, including
...e steel H-frames hung from
...e cantilever of the floor slab
...ove, vertical ducts between
...mes, fixed zone cladding
...nels, variable inserts and
...e horizontal ring duct below
...e perimeter of the first floor
...b; and from the interior
...owing the blockwork fire wall
...hind radiators in casings, and
...novable panels to H-frames
...d skirtings.

to hit a moment in time where the engineers,
dealing with the conditioning of space for
equipment, or apparatus as they called it, were
thinking along the same lines that we were. They
normally had big fans and *massive trunking* from
a central plant going to all ends of the building,
you know; totally inflexible, you couldn't alter it.
I mean you could cut it off, things like that, but
these were isolated, discrete units.[32]

On each floor, horizontal service ducts ran behind the
spandrel panels beneath each window and were sized
for future expansion, a now-common Pearson touch.

Next came the very specialised services for the
NPTE — the emergency generators, the underground
car park and the cable loading and storage system.

The generators and their fuel tanks were housed
at the lowest basement level, 42 feet (12.80 metres)
below ground. A concrete shaft punched its way from
here up through eight floors of the building to outlets
just above the podium, reminiscent of an ocean liner
and necessary to allow fumes to be released through
an array of exhaust pipes.[33] A shaft for the radiation
and dispersal of heat ran from basement to street level,
along with another large enough to permit passage of
a generator set, this being roofed by concrete beams
which were then covered by paving slabs. Above the
generator space were three split-level floors of car
parking (six navigable floors) for around 350 cars
with ramps, lift and stairs and ventilation for normal
and emergency use. Cabling provision included the
enclosure of the existing cable cluster in a concrete
duct, connection to the NPTE and maintenance and
hoisting facilities.

Generally, all penetrations for services were brought
together. This formed three additional, smaller, service
cores in the podium which reserved as much open space
for apparatus, personnel and even cars as possible.

As with much of his work, then, Pearson showed
an intelligence and forethought when arranging
services which, when combined with his siting of the
fixed elements and the spaces these produce, achieved
the maximum usage within the volume available.

Cladding
Pearson had ensured that internal space and services,
especially air conditioning, were responsive to the
building's likely uses. However, this very responsiveness
gave rise to another issue.

Local air handling units could, as noted, be moved
or multiplied, but a supply of air would still be required
for them to function. Conversely, if staff moved into an

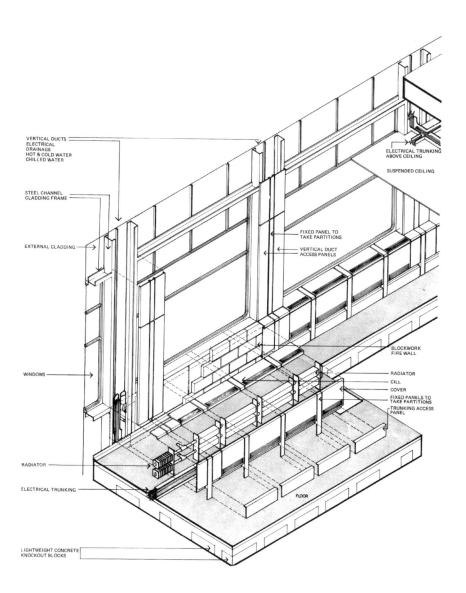

VERTICAL DUCTS
ELECTRICAL
DRAINAGE
HOT & COLD WATER
CHILLED WATER

ELECTRICAL TRUNKING
ABOVE CEILING

SUSPENDED CEILING

STEEL CHANNEL
CLADDING FRAME

FIXED PANEL TO
TAKE PARTITIONS

VERTICAL DUCT
ACCESS PANELS

EXTERNAL CLADDING

BLOCKWORK
FIRE WALL

WINDOWS

RADIATOR
CILL
COVER
FIXED PANELS TO
TAKE PARTITIONS
TRUNKING ACCESS
PANEL

RADIATOR

ELECTRICAL TRUNKING

FLOOR

LIGHTWEIGHT CONCRETE
KNOCKOUT BLOCKS

area previously taken up by apparatus, windows would be welcomed, whilst other internal changes might require alterations to other connections with the outside.

All these scenarios suggested that the exterior of the building should be as adaptable as its interior.

To address this, Pearson and Landau turned once again to the stimulus-response model, applying it this time to exterior walls to produce a "time-skin".[34] In contrast with traditional walls whose apertures and functions are permanent, "setting up a fixed exterior pattern", the time-skin would be able to be modified to reflect changes to the interior.[35]

At the NPTE, exhaustive examination and interpretation of the brief had identified those functions within which might require time-skin walls without: "The particular needs of [its] rooms for large, small or nil amounts of natural light, for different amounts of natural ventilation, areas for grilled mechanical extract or intake, or opening areas required for fire vents."[36]

The pair concluded that walls with "an adaptive capability would therefore provide a new dimension of possibilities" for the special circumstances of this brief and so, in a parallel with the approach taken to layout and services, "capacity for change in plan was extended to the external wall by defining fixed zones and variable zones" there as well.[37] More aphoristically, Pearson described the idea to the present author as taking a adaptable plan and tilting it 90 degrees vertically.

This imaginative theoretical leap was to produce Burne House's most remarkable feature—its innovative cladding.

Pearson proposed a system of prefabricated panels with which the NPTE would be sheathed. Each panel would be of storey height, and thus measure a massive 14 feet five inches (4.42 metres) high and 12 feet six inches (3.86 metres) wide. Each would have a fixed outer zone as its perimeter, but an adaptable inner zone of just over 100 square

feet (nine metres square) or more than half of the panel's total area, a size derived from analysis of likely service demands. This inner zone could be filled with a variety of specialised inserts which would not only reflect but actually facilitate the activities being carried out behind each panel. Thus the list of identified functions described above would now be translated into a range of inserts for the adaptable zone of any panel: solid, opaque inserts, both fixed and openable, simply to seal the exterior; glazed units, also both fixed and openable,

for views; intake and extract louvres for the air handling units; and automatically opening smoke vents for emergencies. These inserts were available in several different sizes and could be fitted in many different combinations within the adaptable zone. The inserts were fully interchangeable and were replaceable at any time after installation.

Now, if apparatus was moved to part of a floor that previously housed staff, the nearest cladding panel's glazed insert could simply be removed and replaced with a louvred insert to permit a relocated air handling unit to function. Staff relocated to a former equipment area could receive windows in the same way.

Daringly, but fully in line with Pearson's and Landau's second evolutionary theory of time-based architecture, this argument also hinted that a building fitted with such panels need not be limited to the functions of its initial occupier; with this amount of adaptability, the building could quite easily cope with a complete change of use. Even without this, as Landau and Pearson stated in ending their article, the potential was enormous.

In keeping with Pearson's aims for the NPTE's visual appearance, though, the cladding would need to fulfil an aesthetic role as well. The panels would automatically generate the bay size for the facades, but the precise arrangements of the inserts had to play their part in the accompanying visual rhythm: "It was essential to create an overall geometry which would accommodate this random pattern in a design of overall elegance but also to maintain this balance as elements changed."[38] The finish and colour of the external panel surfaces would obviously also be important.

This then was the concept — "a sophisticated, lightweight metal skin".[39] The sizeable problem which remained was how to realise it. In the late 1960s, such an advanced cladding system as was being proposed for the NPTE appeared beyond the capabilities of most designers, let alone fabricators.

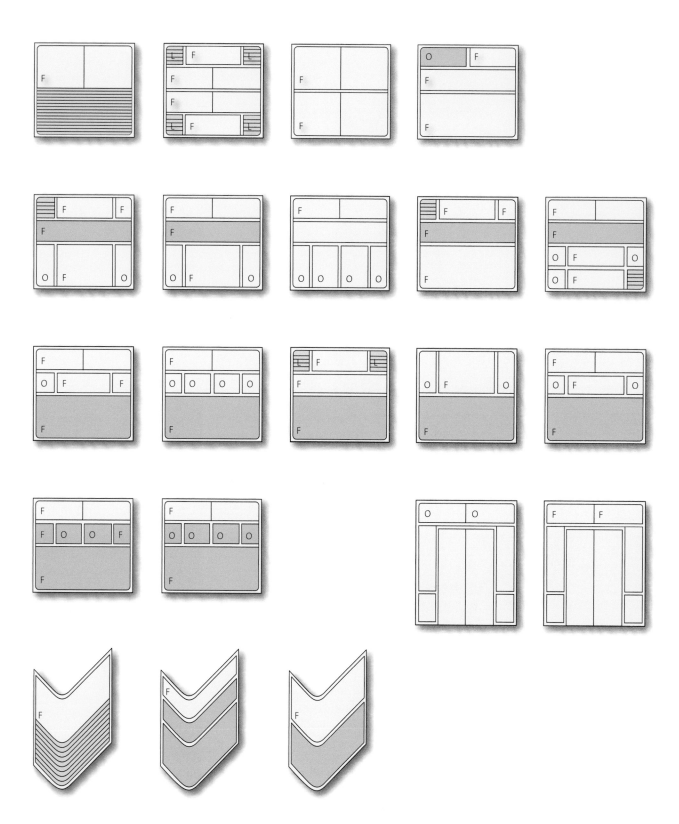

LOUVRES FOR PERM. VENT

 LOUVRES AS AIR INLET/
OUTLET TERMINALS

 FIXED GLASS

 OPENABLE GLASS

F FIXED PANELS

O OPENABLE PANELS

Sheet showing combination options possible with the variable inserts.

Initially Pearson turned to the continent for help, specifically to none other than Prouvé who, having produced a series of cladding systems for buildings such as the CIMT offices in Aubervilliers had, by the late 1960s, an established reputation in this specialism. Pearson had encountered Prouvé's cladding work whilst travelling extensively in France after marrying his second wife. He had especially admired Prouvé's work on the facade of Building V of the Miollis/Bonvin UNESCO complex in Paris, begun in 1967. Pre-fabricated panels of stamped galvanised iron sheet insulated with rock wool featured fixed and opening glazing and were fitted with *brises soleil*. The building itself had curved corners. Later seeing Prouvé's enamelled aluminium sandwich cladding panels for the Erasmus university medical centre, Rotterdam, Pearson felt immediately that the Frenchman might be able to design a cladding panel that combined thinness with lightness, and in the kind of bold approach that he had learned at Manchester wrote to Prouvé to outline the problem.

Prouvé's initial response—a panel using inch-thick steel backed with rubber—met the first criteria but singularly failed the latter, although this is likely to have been a result of Prouvé's experience designing for the tropics, where metal allows for rapid cooling at night. A second attempt, in late 1970, used polyurethane and styrene for insulation, but this proved incompatible with London fireproofing regulations.

Although Pearson even met Prouvé to discuss the issue, ultimately he was forced to look elsewhere, depriving London of a building contribution by an undisputed master. A small Prouvé influence would still find its way into Burne House's eventual cladding solution, though, as will be seen.

In this period of "never-ending variation in the elevation", David Allford suggested louvres set clear of every facade of the NPTE.[40] This would have evoked Prouvé and the work of German architect Egon Eiermann, who was using similar all-round

brises soleil on his buildings including the Bonn parliamentary office tower, 1965–1969, and an administrative and training centre for Olivetti at Frankfurt, begun 1967, where they doubled as maintenance walkways. Pearson eventually rejected this idea as he could not justify such attachments on the northwest and northeast sides of the NPTE where solar gain was absent.

Pearson was concerned that the necessary expertise simply could not be found in Britain, but it was Landau who persuaded Pearson to look to a surprising source for an answer—George Reginald Yeats, the man who had triumphed over Pearson's father in the Harpenden competition decades before and who, as Superintendent of Works, had given Pearson the NPTE job in the first place. Yeats had gone on to a successful career as an architect and had designed one of London's true architectural icons, the Post Office Tower, completed in 1965. That structure had required considerable expertise in technically complex cladding, and the firm which had provided it for Yeats was Crittall Hope, a merger of two concerns known for steel-framed windows for inter-war housing and the special opening windows for the Houses of Parliament, respectively, and which had developed a major "curtain walling and feature fenestration" business for commercial buildings.[41]

Crittall were thus appointed as a sub-contractor to design Burne House's cladding against a performance specification, as with the SCSD school system. The cladding specification was written mainly by Landau and Sidney Watts, a talented director and designer with an architectural ironmonger (something Prouvé would have appreciated) whose knowledge of the performance of metals proved useful. Also involved in this aspect of the project were Shahana Khan and Navin Shah, an Indian-born architect who had come to Pearson through Roy Landau and who had also worked under noted Indian architect BV Doshi. Shah, engaged

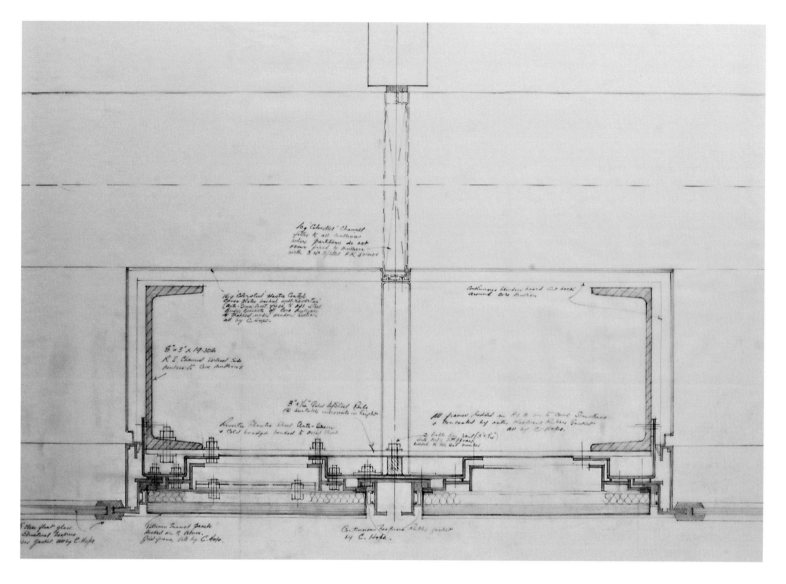

with the team in checking and correcting Crittall's drawings, emphasises that the cladding was "not a tried and tested system" but something very new. Close liaison with panel manufacturer Escol also took place.[42]

The development process was extensive. Over 4,000 design and shop drawings were produced, including many at life size on AO sheets one metre square, and some details were revised a dozen times. Shah states that his team were "keen and meticulous to make sure [the cladding] not only functionally did the job but also visually. [Our goal] was a streamlined, elegant [result]."[43] An early version of the panels featured strongly radiused corners for both the panel and the flexible zone, which Pearson compares to contemporary railway carriages but which yet again references Prouvé. Sharper, more right-angled corners were eventually adopted.

After much effort, a completed design was arrived at for a panel of the composite metal type in which two sheets of metal—here steel—are

pressed to form shallow pans or trays and then placed face-to-face to make a flat box, the interior of which was a rigid board of inert material. The finish of the outside surfaces of the pans provides the interior and exterior treatments for the building without further applied covering, and at NPTE this finish was to be vitreous stove enamelling. This is a process whereby a thin layer of powdered glass is fused to a metal base by firing both at temperatures of around 800° Celsius; the result is an extremely smooth, thin coating, familiar domestically from baths and refrigerator doors but which has many advantages in architectural use including durability, low maintenance and resistance to fire.

Because of size limitations with the zero-carbon steel necessary for vitreous enamelling and the furnace, each cladding panel had to be assembled from smaller sections joint-sealed with polysulphide making the panels for Burne House bespoke in every way, although Pearson was to neatly work

Opposite
Sidney Watt's hand-drawn,
life-size plan section through a
cladding panel junction shows
the detail of mounting and
jointing units.

Above
Artist's impression of the
visitors' entrance with specially-
commissioned reception desk
and seating, all upholstered
in leather.

this necessity into the aesthetics in due course. Fortunately, the complexities of manufacturing the panels were offset somewhat by the adoption of a single panel type for the whole building save the curved items necessary for the corners of the tower and podium.

Importantly for Pearson, coloured enamelling was possible by the addition of various minerals during the firing process, producing a rich, stable colour that would not fade over time. Given the colour eventually used, Pearson's first ideas are perhaps surprising to hear: "My earliest thoughts were to use the colours that were on the Eiffel Tower the last time I saw it, sort of deep Van Dyke brown and a kind of crimson, deep crimson. Railway carriages used to be painted in those colours."[44]

Deep rose and burnt sienna were other possible choices under this scheme, which would in fact also have echoed the domestic Georgian, Victorian and Edwardian buildings in the streets surrounding the

site. Two very different inspirations were to come together to provide the NPTE's eventual colour, however.

Pearson and Landau had recently visited Crittall in Wolverhampton; changing trains at Birmingham and standing on a bridge overlooking that city's new Bull Ring centre, completed in 1965 and designed by James A Roberts, they had been struck by the off-white finish of the Rotunda. Pearson, meanwhile, had a love of the stucco-fronted nineteenth century housing in South Kensington, London where he would later live. A search of the British Standard colour chart found that 08 B 15 Magnolia would replicate the effect both admired, and the NPTE's look was set. Although magnolia is a colour more associated with the suburban semi-detached house than cutting-edge commercial design this choice, combined with the thin lines of the dark-coloured polysulphide sealant needed to join the small panel sections, allowed for a highly sophisticated, carefully modulated visual effect, as Pearson explains:

> I had taken a whole series of photographs [...] of 1840s stucco-fronted classical houses [...] and the shadows were very soft and grey [...] I mean they might be long shadows, but those little mouldings were [in] fine grey shadow, and that's what I tried to do with the black sealant, to create a pattern of slightly greyish darkish colour as a grid. And of course they are all magnolia.[45]

The interchangeable inserts for each panel were sealed with neoprene gaskets, as at the Crown Local Offices. At the NPTE, though, Pearson's concept of the flexible inner zone gave the material a new emphasis, recognition of which would come in due course.

Each panel was attached, via an aluminium intermediary, to an intricately designed steel channel H-frame by right-angled hooks which engaged with horizontal rails at the top and bottom of the frame.

As well as serving as a support structure, this H-frame accepted a vertical aluminium guide groove on its exterior for the building's cleaning cradles to lock into and on the interior formed vertical ducts for services. The H-frame would in turn attach to the structural concrete of the building by cleats, letting the floor slab deflect without adverse strain being transmitted to the cladding. Expansion joints were included. Pearson believes the manner in which the panels were fixed, without the external frame or beading a standard window would have, was another first: "Nobody had used these panels frameless as far as I know."[46] The hook system also allowed the whole panel to be easily removed if required simply by lifting it off of the rails.

Although the internal filling of the panels was now compliant with fire regulations, concrete blockwork was still required behind the spandrel of each to provide additional resistance.

Burne House's cladding system was without doubt a considerable achievement, original in concept, design and fabrication and fulfilling technical and aesthetic criteria equally well. At the earliest possible stage the system proved its worth when functional design changes within the podium required that certain panels be changed during the building's construction, whilst the panels' harmonious arrangement, the unique qualities of the vitreous enamelling and the

colour scheme combined to give Burne House its distinctive finish.

Navin Shah summarises Burne House as a "remarkable project" where creativity and architecture met, and his involvement in it as an "important phase in my career as an architect—the first job I took on."[47]

Staff facilities

Efforts were made to ensure staff facilities at the NPTE were of higher quality than one might expect in such a building. The Post Office had recently introduced new standards for staff accommodation, but Pearson was keen to go beyond this in keeping with his philosophy that: "Buildings should be designed, internally and externally, for the delight, stimulation and convenience of the people who use and visit them."[48]

The result was a remarkably forward-looking approach to designing staff accommodation for such a machine-centric building.

The staff dining room was placed on the top floor of the podium along with a large lounge-cum-games room; both had views onto the animation of the flyover. Smaller tea bars with serveries were sited on some of the tower floors. Female staff were given 'powder rooms' and lockers were available to all. The entrance hall received two items of furniture designed especially for the building and in sympathy with it:

a bank of leather seats for waiting visitors, curved in plan to follow the walls, and a leather-faced reception desk designed almost as a miniature Burne House, with a 'tower' or vertical switch panel perpendicular to a horizontal 'podium'. All corners on both items were radiused. The leather came from Connolly, suppliers to Rolls Royce and other car makers, perhaps another subtle nod toward the automotive aesthetic Pearson developed for this building in its motorised environs.

Colour was specifically employed "to make a large, complex engineering building more comprehensible for the occupants and for visitors".[49] Toilets were differently coloured to aid wayfinding (common practice today), and colour was also used on the apparatus floors, a detail which can be connected to the almost exactly contemporaneous work of Norman Foster at insurance broker Willis Faber & Dumas in Ipswich, Suffolk.

Construction

The effort expended on the design of the NPTE was equalled only by the struggle of construction. Progress can be charted thanks to the superb, disciplined photographic record kept by contractor Taylor Woodrow which meticulously viewed the site from the same four angles every month, including a high-level shot taken mostly, it appears, from the top of Seifert's Metropole Hotel which was being built at the same time.

Ground was cleared in January 1972, before formation of the slurry wall and excavation of the basement. Two major engineering difficulties arose as a direct consequence of the earlier siting decision. First, a method had to be found to prevent 'heave' or upward movement of the Bakerloo Line tunnels once the heavy earth above them was removed. Secondly, the nexus of Post Office cables mentioned previously had to be excavated and enclosed in concrete to create a cable duct, to which the NPTE would be connected.

To safeguard the Underground tunnels, a sheet steel pile wall was inserted just to their south and the earth between it and the slurry wall to the north, with the tunnels beneath, left untouched for nearly two and a half years until May 1974 when the NPTE had reached a height sufficient for its weight to keep the tunnels stable. Only then could the earth above the tunnels be removed and construction of the second phase of the podium begun. The cables had to be excavated — by hand, in cramped conditions and allowing 24 hour access across this part of the site for a neighbouring firm — and a concrete duct cast around them before

the road above was reinstated. It took a year to complete this job alone.[50]

In the final months of 1973, the main service core for the tower was formed in a single 14 day pour using continuously moving shuttering.

By autumn 1974 Taylor Woodrow was keen for the completed structure to be made watertight, and pressured for the cladding to be installed. However, prototype panels had not been produced until November 1972, nearly a year after construction had begun, and final testing was pending. Crittall accordingly refused, although correspondence indicates some impatience on their part too, but Taylor Woodrow went ahead anyway. Navin Shah recalls being telephoned one weekend by the Clerk of Works to be told the cladding was leaking; he called Taylor Woodrow and instructed them to stop installation immediately.

The panels were thereafter subjected to an exhaustive testing regime at the Building Research Station (now BRE) at Garston, Hertfordshire, just north of Watford, where positive and negative pressure loading (wind/suction), thermal, water and corrosion resistance and cleaning requirements were all investigated. This revealed weaknesses at some of the joints, where water penetration occurred in simulated high winds, and Crittall recommended the introduction of metal clips to secure them. Shah refused and describes how these would have spoiled the "very subtle" appearance of the joints, being particularly visible in sunlight.[51] Roy Landau concurred, insisting that none of the various alternative clip examples proposed were acceptable despite assurances from Crittall that their impact would be minimal.

Despite Pearson's team "resisting throughout" this difficult period, time pressures eventually forced the client to direct use of the clips in order to avoid further delay.[52] Pearson was unhappy but had little choice in the matter, and clips were duly fitted.

Nevertheless, as the panels began to be installed in November 1974 — it would be a year before the last was in place — the transformative effect was astonishing. Pearson's full vision was becoming clear. The almost unfathomable complexity of managing such a vast project fell to Pearson too, and he appears to have revelled in the role, shifting effortlessly from calculating the volume of rubbish that the building would generate to ordering a night safe for the car park manager to renewing the building's flagpole licence.

A name was chosen for the new telecommunications centre at around this time. Looking — somewhat ironically, given its planned fate under the full scheme — to the small street dividing the two plots comprising the site, the North Paddington Telephone Exchange became Burne House.

The exterior was eventually finished at the very end of 1976, although it was another four months before the interior was complete and ready for installation of the apparatus. Burne House was finally handed over to the client on 7 July 1977. Photographs show a very happy party in the visitors' entrance hall that day, a superb fully detailed presentation model of the building as executed now occupying the centre of the site planning diorama used years before.[53]

Fittingly, Charles E Pearson was in attendance, and was so proud of his son's achievement that he encouraged Pearson to change the firm's name to reflect this: "Put your own name on it, get some credit for it!" remembers Pearson affectionately.[54]

Reception
Burne House was well received by the contemporary architectural press, critics recognising its intellectual meticulousness and visual beauty.

In a major article for The Architects' Journal, architect Adrian Gale compared Burne House very favourably to Mondial House, examined in the same piece.

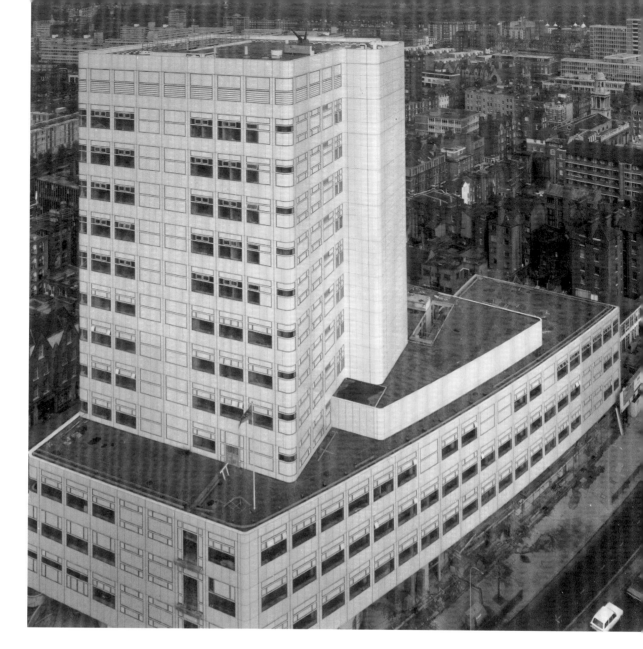

:tober 1976: Cladding complete;
rtical strip in tower facade
vers west shear wall. Note
atment of top storey, loading
ors on west podium and car
rk ramp below.

Gale writes that "Running gently down the ramp of
Marylebone Road, one is aware of an elegant skin
running alongside."[55] Regarding Burne House's exterior,
one slowly becomes aware of the deceptively
simple matrix of differently proportioned
rectangles of solid and void which lie within
the vertical and horizontal framing bands
of vitreous enamel from which the skin is largely
formed. A system of covering the building has
been devised which enables a variety of different
conditions behind the skin to be properly
represented with minimum disruption to the
surface of the building. Two-dimensional only,
the constructional grid slips effortlessly over the
elevation. The quality of this curtain wall grows on
you visit by visit. Thinly veiled shear walls or service
cores hiding just behind the surface are clothed

with ease. Windows, spandrel panels and louvres
slip round a semi-circular corner with an almost
aerodynamic confidence.[56]

Interestingly, Gale describes how the air conditioning
"breathes" through the skin of the building, a striking
echo of Kahn's description of his own Alfred Newton
Richards Medical Research Building, quoted in
Massing, above.[57]

Gale does question whether the aligned vertical
mullions of the panels should have indicated the
presence of structural columns rather than service
runs, citing Ieoh Ming Pei's Mile High Center, Denver,
completed in 1956, whose cladding creates two
separate visual patterns of structure and services,
but praises the "abstract pattern" which results
and states that the "sheer technical elegance and

rne House from the south
th blank service tower wall.
e two vertical bays on the
ft have fresh air grilles for
r control.

excellence of the skin of Burne House transcend [...] any such esoteric inquiry".[58]

Gale concludes his assessment by judging Burne House "an urbane and elegant response to its functional and technological programme" with an exterior "expressive of change that will follow, teaching more when seen close-up [whose] off-white tone [...] could not have been bettered in its urban context".[59]

In a perceptive article for *Building*, architect and former editor of *The Architects' Journal* Colin Davies was equally positive, relating the completed building directly to the brief:

> The most striking feature of the building is the smooth, single-pane, curved-cornered, wrap-around, cream-coloured external skin. If this were an office building, with a straightforward and standardised performance specification, it would be a remarkably slick exercise in glossy lightweight cladding. In this case, however, the performance specification was anything but standardised. The skin is designed to cope neatly and elegantly with a very wide range of requirements.[60]

Davies also discusses in some detail the links to Prouvé, and in addressing Pearson's use of neoprene to seal the inserts pointed out that:

> few [architects] have made use of the fact that the gasket that is so easily 'zipped up' to fix a cladding panel in place can just as easily be unzipped so that the panel can be replaced with another of a different type. Probably for the first time Burne House takes full advantage of this possibility in a comprehensive and complex way.[61]

Saarinen had suggested this possibility for neoprene gaskets at the General Motors Technical Center, but recognition of Pearson as the first to do so at Burne House is valuable.

An anonymous feature in *Building Design* which appeared the year before Burne House was completed described it as "handsome", "stylish" and with "clean good looks", a technical briefing on cladding systems published by *The Architects' Journal* four years and one day after Burne House was handed over speaks of its "finely controlled aesthetic" and the relevant Pevsner guide called Burne House "well detailed" with "ingenious" cladding.[62]

Reappraisal

Today, Burne House maintains its light, unassuming presence above the street markets, schools and homes of Paddington, its polished, unobtrusive skin shifting in colour from bright white to warm orange through the day according to the prevailing light. And yet it also feels more at home than ever in the persisting motor city milieu of the Westway, that same skin seeming to capture the perpetual motion of passing vehicles whipping over its glossy surface like an endless loop of videotape and altering its form as if in tune with the dynamically trafficked roads around it.

Burne House's fluid lines thus pair beautifully with Hamilton's restored and now listed Maintenance Depot, which is actually visible from Burne House, and stand in powerful opposition to the resolutely angular outline of that other iconic neighbour, Trellick Tower by Ernö Goldfinger, with its rectilinear planes and bush-hammered concrete, completed in 1972 and lying further west. The trio highlight the "cinematic experience" provided by navigating the Westway, "a triumphal entry" into the city, visible through what British filmmaker Chris Petit—who featured just this view in the poster for his road movie *Radio On*—calls the "ratio of the windscreen".[63]

For those who do have time to pause, Pearson's cladding displays a consistent, deducible rationale utterly based in the brief and yet also undeniably depicts pleasure in the use of materials simply for

This has become the signature image of Burne House, appearing in articles, brochures for Charles B Pearson Son & Partners and Crittall, the 2004 Pearson centenary exhibition at the AA and, of course, the present work.

their aesthetic effect. It can be read like a book and the functions behind each panel teased out—here a stairway, there a machine room, elsewhere offices—and should our observers compare an older image of the building to what they see today, the story of the changes wrought over time will become clear in the pattern of the panels, which have changed as these functions have changed.

This leads inevitably to the tantalising question that lies at the heart of the Burne House story: its precise position in the lineage of twentieth century buildings with modular, interchangeable cladding.

It may be that further research is required to establish the definitive position, but this author believes that Burne House was the first commercial building in Britain to claim the distinction of a complex, fully adaptable system of this kind.

Certainly a number of buildings were completed around the same time as, or shortly after, Burne House and had panelled cladding systems. Some were also designed to accommodate future change, and one even resembled Burne House at close quarters. Almost all were rapidly feted, and as a result it is often assumed that amongst this group lies a challenger. A detailed examination of these buildings, however, refutes this.

Reliance Controls, Swindon, by Team 4 (Richard Rogers, Su Rogers (née Brumwell), Norman Foster, Wendy Foster (née Cheeseman)), was completed in 1967 and used ribbed metal cladding to efficiently enclose a steel beam and column structure. In the context of the present comparison, however, it was notable only for its capacity for linear expansion. Similarly, although closest to Burne House chronologically and with prefabricated wall and roof units, James Stirling's Olivetti Training Centre, Haslemere (1969–1972) was extendable at a later date but did not employ fully changeable cladding. Foster's Sainsbury Centre for Visual Arts, Norwich, designed

between 1974 and 1976 and opened in 1978, also had extension potential; its cladding housed services between outer and inner walls, as Pearson had done with his Crown Local Offices roofs.

Between 1967 and 1971 Rogers built two houses (the Spender and Rogers houses) and conceived two more (the famous Zip-Up Houses) that used modular cladding on a steel frame; the Spender house in Ulting, Essex was completed in 1969 and featured interchangeable wall panels and windows, but it was a residential building and its cladding is simple.

Rogers did produce a number of panelled semi-industrial buildings from 1967; some were extendible but only one had interchangeable cladding, that for United Oil Products at Tadworth, Surrey, built after Burne House began, in 1973–1974. Rogers' winning entry in the Pompidou Centre competition used solid, translucent and fully glazed exterior panels, but once again this came after Burne House conceptually, in 1971, and was, of course, in Paris.

In 1976 Nicholas Grimshaw completed the Herman Miller Assembly Plant at Bath, whose cladding panels could be swapped as needed, although the late date should again be noted as should the fact that the system is, once more, much simpler than at Burne House. Only a single type of solid and two types of window panel were used, all were monolithic without inserts or variation and there was no linkage to services. Four years later Grimshaw built the BMW Distribution Centre in Bracknell. Here, large white metal panels sealed with neoprene and curved corners produced a visual effect remarkably like Burne House, but again this was not intended to cope with change and was a static system.

Only well into the 1980s did British commercial buildings match Burne House. The differing cladding panels of Rogers' Inmos factory in Newport, Wales, 1980–1982, were designed for standardisation and speed of erection with changeability implied, whilst Grimshaw's Distribution Centre warehouse for Herman Miller in Chippenham, Wiltshire, 1983, now did feature cladding that comprised a fully interchangeable

> kit of parts. Solid panels, fixed windows, opening windows, fire doors, and personnel doors may all be unbolted and moved to any location on a 2.1 x 1.2 metre grid, while the four apertures of each window frame allow the further flexibility of interchanging glass with a vocabulary of secondary components such as external lights, ventilation louvres and components allowing pipe transitions.[64]

It can thus be seen that none of these apparent competitors is able to challenge Burne House, where Pearson out-thought and pre-dated all others.

Why, then, was Burne House's leading position not recognised by critics who otherwise appreciated its inherent technical qualities?

These other works were prestigious private or corporate commissions rather than public sector infrastructure works, and most were designed by architects who were either established 'names' or up and coming future 'stars'. Many used colour and form derived from swagger and nascent postmodernism rather than the reticence and contextual sensitivity displayed by Pearson. All were rendered familiar through the kind of extensive publicity largely denied to Burne House by virtue of its arrival as a significant part of the public communications network during a time of increased terrorism on the British mainland.[65] All these factors combined to exclude Burne House from its true place in the popularly examined and accepted canon of flexibly clad buildings — as progenitor.

In many ways, though, Pearson's masterwork has regained some of that lost kudos in recent years, and now demands the fresh look that the present

work attempts to provide. More striking still — and eminently right — is the survival and, indeed, late flourishing of "this shy and retiring building" when seen against a variety of its contemporaries.[66]

Burne House's fellow telecommunications centres have suffered. Mondial House was demolished in 2006–2007, less than 20 years after Prince Charles decried its appearance as a dreadful word processor, whilst, at the time of writing, Keybridge House was attracting media coverage after complaints from local residents over its rundown appearance; design commentator Stephen Bayley described it as "BT's shameful secret" and passed on speculation that demolition would occur when contracts and leases permit.[67] Curiously, Pearson notes that the externalised service ducts employed on Keybridge House as visible, Kahnian "formal elements" were actually its downfall; they proved to be either too small or too large when new services were required and this, together with the heavy use of concrete in the building, resulted in the costs of alteration to accommodate the new telecommunications apparatus being ten times those incurred at Burne House for the same task.[68]

Of those much-admired 'flexible' buildings, the panelling on the Sainsbury Centre failed rapidly and had to be replaced in the 1980s whilst the Reliance Controls factory was demolished in 2000, albeit that this was an expected part of its original concept.

Cladding systems designed by Prouvé have also, ironically, been found wanting. A 2002 report for UNESCO on Miollis/Bonvin Building V describes water leakage, draughts and heat loss although Prouvé's facade was still considered of sufficient architectural merit for a €3.2 million programme of repairs to be proposed rather than replacement. The streamlined facade he designed for Jean de Mailly's and Jacques Depusse's Tour Nobel, 1964–1967, in Paris's La Défense business district, regarded by

Previous pages
Something of the Chrysler building
and other machine-age skyscrapers
of New York is caught in this image
with its disolving corners.

Left
A recent view of the southwest
corner showing alterations at
mid-height near the corner.

many as the apogee of his facade designs, was replaced in 2001–2003 due to its use of asbestos. The acclaimed Institute de l'Environnement, also in Paris, designed by R Jolly in 1969 and with enamelled panel cladding by Prouvé that is remarkably similar to that of Burne House, has been demolished.

Burne House has even outlasted the three other blocks in Westminster Council's crossroads plan, all of which have been forced to adapt to change in ways often betraying the original artistic intention. Seifert's Century House exemplifies this, having been completely remodelled and reclad in the late 1980s in a postmodern vein. His Metropole Hotel has had its mosaic cladding overpainted and been extended twice, unsympathetically. In 2007, Paddington Green police station (by J Innes Elliot, Surveyor to the Metropolitan Police) was reported to be marked for replacement as it proves inadequate for its role as a high security facility.

Yet none of this is surprising. All of it shows that the time factor in architecture has been as critical as Pearson and Landau believed it would be, and that only buildings designed with this in mind will prevail. Burne House was, others were not. As has been seen, changes to Burne House were required even during construction, and the design responded. Within a few years of completion, the new digital exchange equipment was installed at lesser cost than elsewhere; raised floors and deeper suspended ceilings followed, easily accommodated by the greater-than-usual floor heights. By the mid-1990s three quarters of the main spaces had new technology put in place and more than a dozen new air handling units had been fitted. The cladding has been cleaned only once.

Nearly ten years after Burne House was handed over, Pearson and Navin Shah returned to the building at the request of BT to conduct a maintenance management survey of the building:

I was asked by the boss of London telecommunications, prior to privatisation to assess the condition of BH. We spent a year crawling all over the building. There were few defects. We made a library of drawings, manufacturers' information, schedules for maintenance, budgets and so on. I do not believe any building has had such a thorough investigation a decade after completion.[69]

Given the joint influences of Saarinen's car plants, Prouvé's various transport inspirations and its immediate environs, as well as its innately mechanical nature, it is satisfyingly apposite that this was termed a study of Burne House's "performance", as though it were a highly tuned racing car.[70]

The survey placed Burne House on a sound footing for the future, in any role. It would not prove difficult to convert Burne House to a highly serviced office block, the cladding changing as needed. Indeed, additional kinds of inserts could be designed for as-yet-unknown services and purposes, a perfect exemplar of Pearson's and Landau's radical evolutionary theory. As Pearson comments, self-effacingly, Burne House was planned "like a warehouse... it can be used for anything".[71]

This comfortable fitness for alternate future uses might turn out to be Burne House's most important feature.

In the early twenty-first century, commercial buildings are changing tenants at a rapid and increasing rate. The flight to new and more cost-effective city quarters, the growing market in serviced office space for very short-term use and market volatility have all contributed to a much faster cycling of building occupation. In such a climate, adaptability will mark out the fittest buildings whilst those which cannot adapt will suffer the ultimate fate beyond vacancy — demolition, something which has already afflicted buildings less than 20 years old in the City of London.[72]

As early as 1995 Richard Rogers himself acknowledged this: "A building that is a financial market today may need to become an office in five years, and a university in ten. A building that is easy to modify has a longer useful life, and uses its resources more efficiently."[73]

Rogers had completed a speculative building in 1992 in London's regenerating Dockland that addressed the issue. Pre-let by the client developers to information provider Reuters and used as their secure data centre, the building was designed to accommodate both staff and equipment and to be flexible enough to change between those functions:

> The building requires a high degree of artificial servicing. The internal space is divided between offices and plant rooms filled with computers, and is designed to accommodate future rearrangement and heavy machinery. An interchangeable cladding system of solid and glazed panels reflects the interior's inherent flexibility.[74]

More striking even than this similarity to Burne House is its three external, detached service towers, along with a fourth containing the principal lift bank. For Pearson, it proved to be a rueful case of déjà vu:

> When I saw the design for the Reuters building I knew I had been there before [in] my original proposal for maximum flexibility of the working area with the fixed elements of circulation located outside to give ultimate freedom of internal re-arrangement over time for the equipment.[75]

In just one respect has time proven to be Burne House's enemy rather than its ally.

Telecommunications technology has progressed even further and faster than predicted and neither of the intended additional stages were, or will ever be, built.[76] The east façade of Burne House's podium remains permanently scarred with 'temporary' corrugated metal sheeting, a community housing scheme now occupying the site originally earmarked for an extension. Burne Street remains, albeit truncated by the podium; a pedestrian through-route is preserved to Marylebone Road. To the west, Leslie Green's 1907 Edgware Road Underground station remains, as does its neighbouring pub of around the same period. It might be regarded as somewhat ironic that Pearson, an enthusiast for technology, would find its very march thwarting expansion of his greatest work.

Conclusion

To create Burne House, Pearson took new theories, not universally accepted, unbuilt but highly original schemes and experience of designing in to a building as much adaptability as possible, via a combination of structural allowance, clustering of sub-systems and service design and planning. To this he added a unique cladding system with leading-edge technology that mediated between all of these elements and helped generate a visual form of unmatched poetry that remains wholly appropriate for an area attracting architecture optimised for viewing at speed. Compressing all of this in the pressure vessel of the mind, he realised, with his team, an extraordinary building in extraordinary circumstances.

Burne House is also the embodiment of Pearson's process-driven approach to design, proven in an unusually testing atmosphere in which a complex three-way exchange—Landau's "richer concept of interaction"—yielded a positive result for all.[77]

For Pearson, Burne House was "the centre of my work".[78] For Navin Shah, it was "conceptually the best" of the three new central London centres.[79] For English Heritage, it has been a provocation; although listing has been consistently declined, the organisation has acknowledged that the "interest of its planning and cladding systems [were] not by any means entirely understood" even in the mid-1990s.[80] For others, it has been an inspiration, as a fully mature, fully worked out solution to a universal architectural problem. It has never outstayed its welcome and has continuing value today, suggesting that Burne House's time may yet come.

1   MP, in conversation with the author, 22 January 2008.

2   An experimental digital exchange designed to prove the new technology had been set up in London as early as 1962.

3   The first operational digital exchange entered public service in Britain under the name System X in September 1980; the last main electro-mechanical exchange closed in July 1990.

4   Morgan, TJ *The utilisation of large telecommunications buildings*, The Institution of Post Office Electrical Engineers, September 1967.

5   The road and rail links in the area had already resulted in many corporate, academic and other institutions making Marylebone Road their home over the years, such as retailer Woolworth, oil giant Castrol, the Society of Friends, the Methodist Missionary Society, the historic and scientific research arm of Henry Wellcome's pharmaceutical business, Cambridge University Press, the Philological College and the Royal Academy of Music.

6   The IPOEE paper includes a diagram showing stage two to the west and stage three to the east, although a later brochure on the Burne House project produced by Pearson reverses this.

7   Pearson relates how Seifert first promoted a residential scheme, in line with the original requirement for the site, but changed this to a luxury hotel (originally the Metropole, now the Hilton London Metropole) once permission appeared certain. Ironically the hotel does now contain long-term residential suites.

8   MP, in conversation with the author, 16 October 2007.

9   By the mid-1980s, micro-electronics allowed the writing and typesetting of text to be computerised and easily divorced physically from the printing of the final product, with the two operations able then to fit in smaller, more conventional buildings.

10 MP, email to the author, 19 January 2008.

11 Michael Pearson Associates practice brochure, c. 1996; MP, in conversation with the author, 22 July 2008.

12 MP, letter to Paul Hyett, 13 July 2003.

13 Document supporting Pearson International's entry in the Tête Défense competition, Paris, October 1982. See chapter 7 International Works.

14 & 15 MP, in conversation with the author, 17 February 2008.

16 Kahn, Louis I *Louis I Kahn: Complete Works 1935–74*, Heinz Ronner with Sharad Jhaveri and Alessandro Vasella, Westview Press, 1977. Ironically, given his interest in science and his admiration for the Alfred Newton Richards building, Pearson has never designed a laboratory, although he came close in the mid-1990s with a scheme planned for Reading, Berkshire.

17 MP, in conversation with the author, 17 February 2008.

18 MP, letter to the author, 7 June 1994.

19-21 MP, in conversation with the author, 17 February 2008.

22 MP, *A note on our attitude to design*, Pearson promotional text, 9 May 1977.

23 MP, in conversation with the author, 17 February 2008.

24 MP, in conversation with the author, 16 October 2007; MP, in conversation with the author, 12 February 2008; MP, in conversation with the author, 17 February 2008.

25 MP, *A note on our attitude to design*, promotional text.

26 Regrettably the whole of this garden was removed in the early 2000s, presumably on security and maintenance grounds, and replaced with cobbled paving and saplings.

27-29 MP, in conversation with the author, 16 October 2007; MP, in conversation with the author, 12 February 2008.

30 MP, in conversation with the author, 16 October 2007; although Westminster Council closed the market c. 2007 because of lack of demand for pitches (remaining pitches were relocated to nearby Church Street market), traders still gather unofficially.

31 Pearson practice document, date and purpose unknown.

32 Although their packaged air conditioning units combined the two stages of water chilling and air cooling in one unit; MP, in conversation with the author, 1 March 2008.

33 The generator area is actually referred to as the engine room in some plans.

34-36 Royston Landau, MP, "A note on an architecture of time", *Architectural Design*, August, 1971.

37-39 Ibid; document supporting Pearson International's entry in the Tête Défense competition

40 MP, in conversation with the author, 1 March 2008.

41 The Post Office Tower cladding included double-glazed window panels with 'anti-sun' external glass, opening inner glass and aluminium *brises soleil* in the 250mm gap between the two; Crittall Construction brochure, c. 1980.

42 & 43 Navin Shah, in conversation with the author, 1 February 2008.

44 & 45 MP, in conversation with the author, 19 February 2008.

46 MP, in conversation with the author, 17 February 2008.

47 Navin Shah, in conversation with the author, 1 February 2008.

48 & 49 MP, *A note on our attitude to design*, promotional text.

50 For a full account of the difficulties encountered in digging Burne House's foundations, readers are referred to Jerry Gosney, "Double Dig Solves PO Puzzle", *Contract Journal*, 6 February 1975, from which much of this section derives.

51 & 52 Navin Shah, in conversation with the author, 1 February 2008.

53 This model and the diorama survive in Pearson's care; the model was rejected for exhibition by the Royal Academy.

54 MP in conversation with the author, 17 February 2008; see *List of projects and information on sources* for more on the various names of the practice and the significance of 1977 in the story. Charles E Pearson died in 1982.

55-59 Gale, Adrian *Mondial House Burne House*, *The Architects' Journal*, 16 February 1977.

60 & 61 Davies, Colin "Fair exchange", *Building*, 6 May 1977.

62 "Smooth talkin'", *Building Design*, 8 October 1976; Alan Brookes, Martyn Ward, "The art of construction 2.3 Sheet metal claddings Part 1 The range of systems", *The Architects' Journal*, 8 July 1981; Nikolaus Pevsner, Bridget Cherry, *Buildings of England London: Volume 1 The Cities of London and Westminster*, Penguin, 1981.

63 de Rijke, Alex, *Westway, On the Road: the art of engineering in the car age*, Catherine Croft ed., Hayward Gallery/Arts Council/The Architecture Foundation, 1998; David Lee of Maunsell, quoted in Self, Will, "Way-out Westway", *ES Magazine*, May 1993; Petit, Chris, "The road to everywhere", *100 Road Movies*, Wood, Jason, London: BFI, 2007.

64   *Herman Miller Warehouse, Chippenham, 1983, World Architecture*, May 1993.

65   Burne House was covered by the Official Secrets Act when built; Pearson was warned against talking to the press. Increasing concern over security led to the installation of bullet-resistant glass in the visitors' entrance and protective grilles over the planters during construction. Even the site notice board describing the project was ordered to be removed. Correspondence shows that although the client relaxed its embargo for the opening as a sign of goodwill, within a month the decision was made to halt all future publicity for security reasons. Pearson was actively prevented from including plans of Burne House in his submission for the RIBA regional awards in 1980. Attempts by the author to visit Burne House in the 1990s failed, whilst more recent events in the capital and elsewhere are, to say the least, unlikely to lead to a change in the situation.

66   MP, letter to the author, 7 June 1994.

67   Bayley, Stephen "Is this the ugliest office in Britain?", *The Observer*, 30 December 2007.

68   MP, in conversation with the author, 22 January 2008; as will be seen later in the present work, Pearson went on to work closely with BT, the PO's successor, on a range of London telecommunications projects over 13 years and thus was very familiar with its estate.

69   MP, email to the author, 23 December 2007.

70   Michael Pearson Associates practice brochure, c. 1996.

71   MP in conversation with the author, 16 October 2007.

72   Hamilton House, part of the Broadgate development, was completed c. 1988 but demolished c. 2002 and replaced by 10 Exchange Square (SOM, 2004); Crosby Court (38 Bishopsgate) opened in 1985 but was demolished 2006–2008 for construction of the Bishopsgate tower, known officially as the Pinnacle and unofficially as the helter skelter (Kohn Pedersen Fox, projected for completion in 2012).

73   Rogers, Richard, "The imperfect form of the new", *The Independent*, 27 February 1995.

74   Rogers Stirk Harbour + Partners website, 3 February 2008.

75   MP, letter to the author, 7 June 1994.

76   Pearson confirms that, had they been so, they would have been clad in the same manner as stage one.

77   Royston Landau, "Thinking about architecture and planning – a question of ways and means", *Architectural Design*, September 1969.

78   MP, in conversation with the author, 17 February 2008.

79   Navin Shah, in conversation with the author, 1 February 2008.

80   The present author has attempted to have Burne House listed twice in the last 15 years; Elain Harwood, *Burne House, Bell Street, Westminster Inspector's Advice print*, English Heritage, 2002.

7

International
Works

By early 1973, as the Ewens were enjoying their new studio and Burne House was climbing out of the Paddington soil, Britain had been suffering inflation and industrial unrest for some time. Public expenditure cuts were soon announced, altering the commissioning landscape for many architects almost immediately. Across the Atlantic the dollar was falling and, later that year, as principal victim of Arab oil producers' embargo of countries supporting Israel in the October War, the economy of the United States was depressed even further.[1]

Neither were places for a maturing architect to find work and Pearson consequently took his career in a wholly new direction, designing over the next ten years an extraordinary number and variety of healthcare, educational and commercial schemes across the Middle East, Africa, South America, India and continental Europe.

Although the works from this period would ultimately be confined to paper by some of the same capricious circumstance, they are as important to a full understanding of Pearson's architecture as the executed buildings examined so far.

Despite the risks presented by "political instability, exchange control restrictions on exporting fees and the high costs of ensuring a presence [abroad] when projects are being commissioned", Pearson clearly relished the opportunity.[2] Writing during this period, he ebulliently explained that

> the delights and responsibilities of working overseas are enormous because there are few rules to prop up design judgements and responsibility cannot be abdicated. I remember starting a project and asking a member of the client's committee about local building regulations. "I am the building regulations. I will answer all your questions", he said. One is left to find appropriate standards from all the mass of codes and regulations from the industrialised nations

and interpret them with a logic which cannot usually be applied in their country of origin. This gives a very direct relationship with the client and enables the design process to proceed at a speed rarely achieved since the days of the early nineteenth century engineers or the presentation to the Grand Master of the design and model for Valetta [sic] after three working days.[3]

Such speedy progress was not restricted even by the need now to lead much larger teams of specialists, including local architects with whom the practice often partnered for these jobs. Significantly, this requirement took Pearson's longstanding interest in, and contact with, international designers a logical step forward and honed another facet of his character.

This was not a homogenous marketplace. Pearson was careful to draw a distinction between those countries who had seen the beneficial effects of the embargo's price rises and "the populous developing countries unsupported by the super affluence of oil wealth", and shaped his efforts accordingly.[4] This nuanced approach was fundamental to Pearson's international practice, essentially carrying the sensitivity to client, end users and local conditions displayed previously to the level of an entire culture.

Pearson down-plays his overseas works, describing them as "lesser research projects", but a depth and breadth of thought, often extraordinary complexity of planning and relentless focus on local context mean they more than warrant scrutiny, and naturally his established concern with incorporating change through adaptability and flexibility and original approach to service provision remain.[5] That the schemes live solely in model photographs, drawings and sketches simply gives these a greater role in the current analysis, along with Charles E's superb perspectives, painting a compelling picture of this Edwardian thriving into the 1970s despite

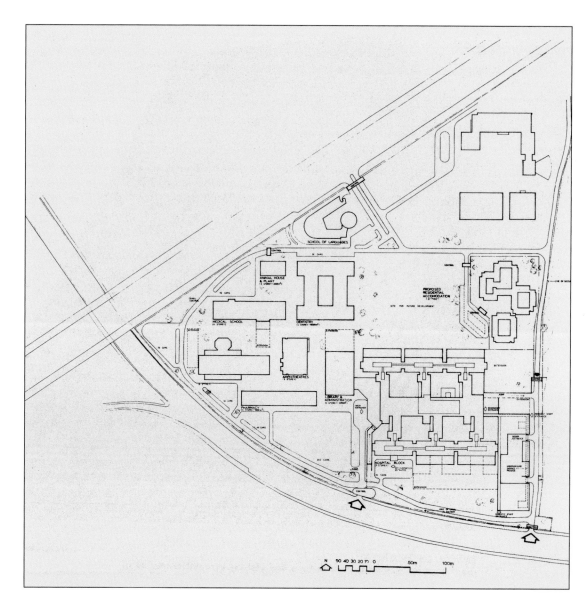

developing tensions within the partnership which
would eventually cause its break up during this
period (see List of projects and sources).

This phase of Pearson's career is therefore no less
stimulating to explore.

Hospitals
The hospital as a building type exerted a particular
pull. It gave wide rein for the conception, development
and deployment of ideas of change, in part due to the
inherently transient nature of medical technology.
This is an obvious similarity to the telecommunications
equipment issue which was the main driver at Burne
House. It was also a field in which user need was, by
definition, paramount.

Pearson had also become concerned at the role
of the architect:

> I was fed up with [others] setting the strategic
> parameters of how units, departments were
> going to be planned, so the private architect was
> just a, you know, hack technician converting
> it into a building. I wanted to be part of the
> strategic action.[6]

Pearson had also met and befriended Howard
Goodman, architect at the Department of Health
& Social Security, and his colleague Raymond Moss
when guest-editing *The Architectural Review*'s
"Preview", and had visited hospitals in the United
States just as Charles B had done.

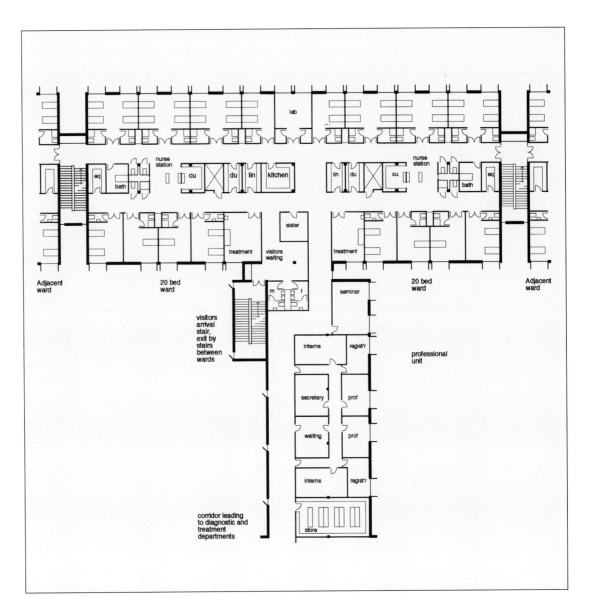

Accordingly, when the chance came to design a new teaching hospital in the Syrian capital, Pearson seized it. Typically, offer and acceptance were unusual; a Syrian representative arrived in London at the British Consultants Bureau, to which Pearson was attached, looking for an architect, but

> [other firms] weren't interested because Syria was politically out of bounds after the '67 war and also its credit rating at ECGD, which was the government insuring agency for projects overseas, was D, and it only goes from A to D, and I thought "whoopee, it must be different, I'll go and have a look at it" and of course I got the job, I only had competition from the French.[7]

The University Teaching Hospital, Damascus was to be the start of a sequence of hospital projects which would see Pearson take on the mantle of his father and grandfather but also expand his own theories in this specialised field. Damascus also set the pattern for other international jobs with its multi-disciplinary teamwork and close reference to local tradition.

After an initial ministerial request for a "1,000 bed tall building as a monument to impress foreign visitors", the brief as finally defined in 1974 was for a 640 bed hospital, an education and training facility and staff residences, to be attached to the University of Damascus and its medical faculty which dated back to 1901, taught exclusively (and uniquely) in Arabic and thus attracted students from across the Middle East.[8]

DAMASCUS

Damascus is at 34°30' N about 80 kilometres east of Beirut at an elevation of 600 metres on the plateau of the Syrian desert close to mountains on its east and north sides. The climate has a hot dry summer, short spring and autumn, and a cool winter.

Summer midday temperatures can rise above 30° C and night time temperatures may go below comfort levels at any time of the year. Humidity remains low throughout the summer. There is little rainfall. Dust and sand storms can cause problems and protection is required from very strong northwest winds.

Winter shade temperatures tend to be below comfort levels. Midday sunshine can be pleasant but the sky is more frequently covered. Heating of buildings is required for five months of the year.

Walls and roofs have a high thermal mass, taking more than 12 hours to absorb or release heat. Courtyards act as cool air reservoirs in summer. Solar gain is reduced by white coloured external walls reflecting rays of the sun and by shading from deciduous trees.

External walls have small openings at high level. Courtyards have openings at 40 per cent of the wall area. Warm air from rooms rises in ducts to exhaust at roof level. The diagnostic and treatment areas are largely supplied with cooled air. Both systems take in cool air at low level in courtyards running over pools of water to increase the humidity for greater comfort. Whilst the humid tropics require a flow of air over the body for comfort, this is not required in these hot dry conditions.

Visitors provide food and laundry for patients. Some six visitors per patient can be expected each day. Say, a total of over 3,500. This number of people could not be transported vertically in a high-rise building by lift without the experience of long waiting times, aggravated by maintenance problems and power failures. So it led to the insertion of an entrance ramp to a mezzanine, over and separated from hospital traffic, leading to a stair to each ward with a maximum rise of one and a half flights. Exit from the wards is then to ground level down stairs at the end of each ward and though a one-way turnstile.

The wards can be administered as 20 bed or 40 bed units. Bed bays and rooms are arranged along external walls with a centre spine of services and ancillary rooms. Connected to the centre of this building is a professional unit for the staff and medical students, forming a T shape plan. This teaching area then forms the route between the wards and the diagnostic and treatment building, arranged on two floors as a wide, adaptable area capable of future change.

The main engineering services run on the roof of the hospital. Each T building has its own direct water supply with storage tanks, and direct electricity supply, stand by generator and fuel supply.

Ring mains give alternative back up. Fan units are also located on the roof. Similar systems provide for the diagnostic and treatment building. This allows for major maintenance or replacement without disturbing occupied rooms, and if one building has a failure it should not affect others.

Michael Pearson

Although the client preferred the prestige of a tower, which the French design duly provided, Pearson demurred. The practice had experience of these in Britain and had come to realise their weaknesses, especially for larger hospitals. Pearson "Argued that [...] tall buildings would not adapt to change and have vertical transportation problems", the latter compounded in Damascus by maintenance questions and the reliability of the local power supply.[9]

Pearson's more operationally efficient and cost-effective concept comprised three parallel blocks of just three storeys, determined as the optimal size for efficient pedestrian movement without reliance on lifts, which were provided but only for some patient transport and senior staff. The two outer blocks held the wards and were split into three self-contained units, each separated by a narrow junction containing the stairs. Each of these units plugged into the central 'spine' block, which housed the diagnostic and treatment functions, via three-storey links comprising offices and seminar rooms for professors and students, giving a series of T-shaped blocks interspersed with courtyards.

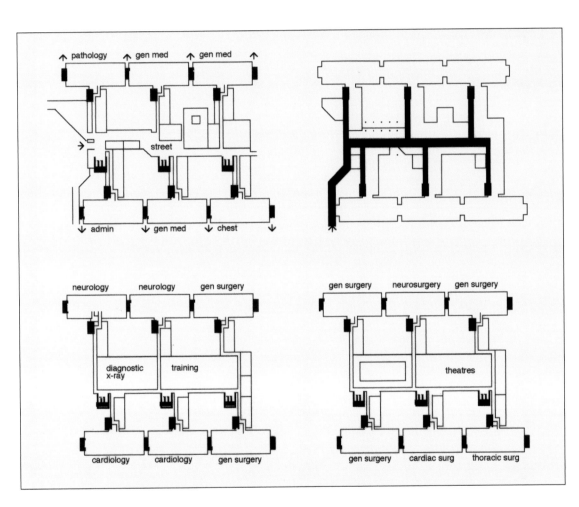

Beyond this succinct arrangement, subtle details emerge. Borrowing from Western practice, wards were arranged on the then-popular racetrack principle, with perimeter beds around a core of utility rooms, and were split by medical discipline, allowing concentration of patient care and student learning. The majority of surgical patients were located on the same floor as the operating theatres. A maximum of just two flights of stairs separated all rooms, and only a third of people making journeys were predicted to need even one flight to reach

their destination. In this, Pearson had a number of precedents to draw on including the Pentagon, headquarters of the United States Department of Defense; though the largest office building in the world at the time it was completed in 1943, its few floors, ingenious layout and use of ramps and escalators ensured a maximum journey time of minutes between any two points.[10]

A key part of Pearson's design was the separation of circulation routes within the hospital. Staff and patients entered at ground floor level and used a

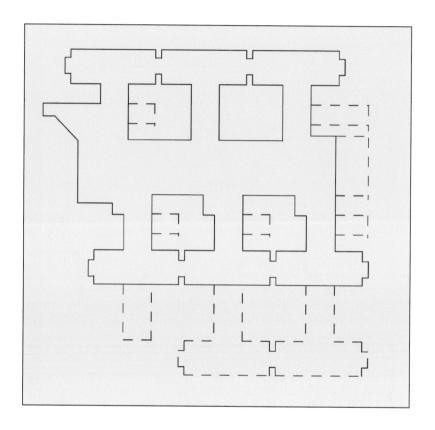

Right
Possibilities for future extensions.

Opposite
Sections through the building
from an original drawing.
Note the visitors' mezzanine,
underground emergency
department and air raid shelter,
and on the roofs, the plant rooms.

generous internal 'street' running through the spine
block to access the rest of the building. The Syrian
custom of relatives giving not only comfort but
also practical support such as food and clothing
created more visitor traffic than at a Western
hospital, however, implying a more imaginative
approach for visitors.[11]

From the pavement a gentle ramp led to a dedicated
mezzanine level extending into the hospital, paralleling
the internal street. Spurs ran through the link blocks
and into the wards to separate visitor stairs. Not
only did this keep the public apart from staff and
patients until beds were reached, but the flow was
also one-way, exit being via the stairs between ward
units to turnstiles in the grounds. In this elegant
harmonisation of architecture with user need lies a
capsule critique of Pearson's work.

Climate control was organic to the architecture,
a result of Pearson recognising the limited availability
of skilled labour that would render fitting air

conditioning throughout the hospital inappropriate
and thence looking to what was possible through the
disposition and design of the buildings themselves.

Pearson confirms "We were concerned about
solar gain, air movement, insulation", but each
obtained in differing degrees in different countries.
Again, a nuanced approach was necessary.[12]

In Damascus, solar gain was the principal issue
in summer (heating was actually required in the
winter months). Wards were aligned east–west with
no windows facing west, minimising solar gain in
the long afternoons; planted gardens were provided
for shade (and views). The small, deep courtyards
acted as cold air reservoirs at night to aid cooling
in the day. Conversely, the buildings' low-rise
nature allowed sunlight to penetrate rooms in the
cold winter period, for which central heating was
provided. The densely-planned spine block gave
minimal surface area to heat or cool, although air
conditioning was provided here.

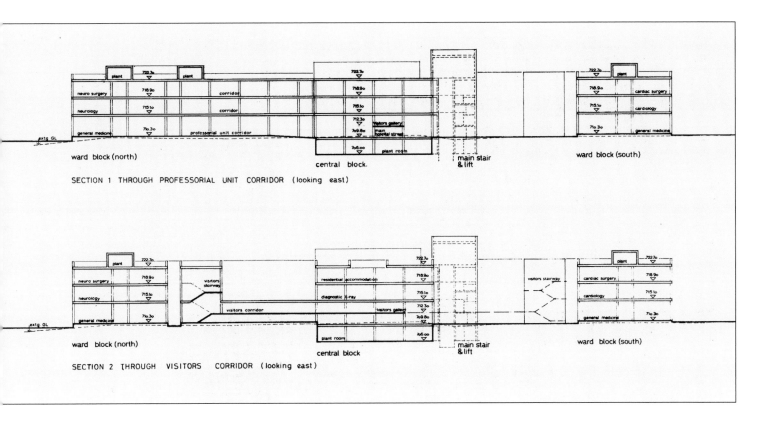

SECTION 1 THROUGH PROFESSORIAL UNIT CORRIDOR (looking east)

ward block (north)   central block.   main stair & lift   ward block (south)

SECTION 2 THROUGH VISITORS CORRIDOR (looking east)

ward block (north)   central block   main stair & lift   ward block (south)

Each T-block and the spine were independently serviced to reduce the impact of plant failure. Highly concentrated services were supplied to rooms from ring mains on the roofs, just as at the Crown Local Offices and Burne House and with the same advantages plus ease of access and emission of noise away from wards.

The kitchen, workshops and laundry were grouped in a separate single-storey 'industrial zone' which minimised disruption when replacing equipment. Teaching and staff accommodation was provided in separate buildings elsewhere on the campus. A reminder of the prevailing atmosphere was the placement of the casualty department in the basement with an air raid shelter next to it; disquietingly, the roof was designed to take the load of the above-ground floors collapsing onto it. Similar sensitivities required Pearson to assure the client in writing over sub-contractors working in Israel.

Structural columns were placed at 6.6 metre centres to create large open spans within which

moveable partitions formed the rooms. In places columns were omitted for even more freedom. Additional patients for a particular ward could be accommodated simply by placing them in adjacent T-blocks; wards could change function, aided by the moveable partitions, and teaching spaces could be given over to medical use if required. Space was retained on the site for expansion when needed, the low-rise design simplifying connection to existing buildings.

Exterior walls were originally to be of pre-cast concrete pieces describing a series of shallow arches, as designed by Anglo-Italian architect Roland Paoletti during a spell with Pearson. Known today for his role as chief architect of London Underground's acclaimed Jubilee Line Extension,1990–1999, and, prior to that, his work on Hong Kong's mass transit system, Paoletti is a near contemporary of Pearson and trained with him at Manchester for a time before working for Basil Spence and Italian architect-engineer-contractor Pier Luigi Nervi. Paoletti is also,

The concept for visitors' flow is seen in action in these superb illustrations by Charles E Pearson. A distant view from the south west clearly shows the pedestrian ramp; this connects to a mezzanine then leads into the hospital overlooking the glazed lobby.

co-incidentally, a nephew of Pearson's architecture school head, the late Professor Cordingley.

Paoletti's solution, though handsome and resembling the facade treatment of Spence's University of Sussex buildings of 1959 onwards, posed practical difficulties:

> I didn't think that it suited [being of] high-performance pre-cast concrete—we needed something that could be built in concrete block [as] they didn't have the technology to do that. They were pre-fabricated units, they had to be. They would have had to be made abroad and shipped in, the cost would have been enormous. Really, we did the simplest of structures— concrete slabs and blockwork.[13]

Architecture is often identified as the work of a named individual—not least in the title of the present work— but this is of course often wholly misleading. As design leader at Damascus, for example, Pearson created, organised and managed a team which included David Gray, a man who was to become a collaborator of Pearson's on many of his hospitals and who brought a very special contribution to their design.

As a surgeon, Gray was involved in a tragic incident which led to a shift in career:

> [He] started at Guy's [hospital], Guy's tower, and he operated on a girl['s] tonsils, and she'd gone back to the ward, and because of the lifts they couldn't get her back up to the theatres fast enough and she died [...] And that upset him so much he stopped practicing as a surgeon, and [after various posts abroad] went back to the department of heath for six years as a medical planner.[14]

Pearson met Gray during the fee bid for Damascus, and a "marvellous" working relationship was born. Pearson considers him "a kindred soul", explaining

C.E. Pearson '75

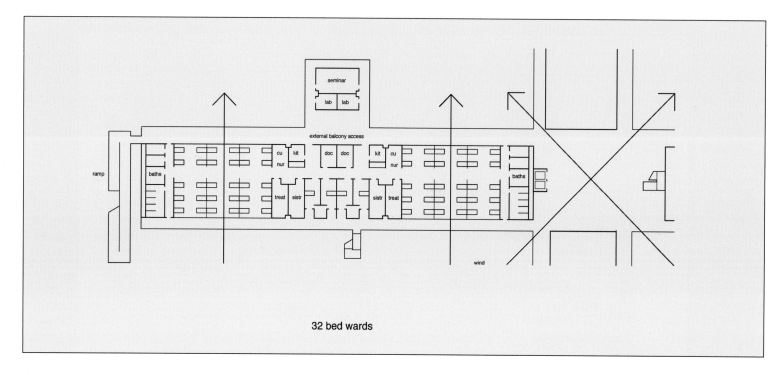

seminar

lab | lab

external balcony access

ramp

baths

cu | kit | doc | doc | kit | cu
nur | nur

treat | sistr | sistr | treat

baths

wind

32 bed wards

University Teaching Hospital,
Ilorin. A typical ward plan
showing the wide external
corridors for sun shading
with ramps at far ends, wind
movement across bed bays and at
open circulation junctions where
stairs and lifts are located, and a
central projecting seminar room
with two adjacent laboratories.
Note vertical service ducts,
accessible from corridors.

how "We sparked off each other; I would do
something and say what he was talking about was
rubbish, and vice versa."[15] Gray helped formulate the
detailed design for Damascus:

> He could find out the records of what they had
> and what they needed and what it cost, work
> out the departmental requirements, put areas
> to it, give a total area for the hospital and give
> it a budget price and work out annual running
> expenses in four weeks.[16]

Gray was also a hugely credible link between Pearson
as architect and the medical profession as clients
during what Gray termed "interactive briefing and
design" sessions in which the design team explained
outline sketches to users, who would then respond.[17]
Seemingly obvious, this actually telescoped the then
standard British practice of briefing followed by sketch

followed by discussion. The use of drawings as a basis
for debate, also a Pearson preference, should be noted.

Pearson devoted four years to Damascus—
whose budget of £27 million (c. £125 million today) he
also managed—before contractor financing problems
caused its abandonment. It proved a signal experience,
however (in every sense, the Yom Kippur/Ramadan
conflict beginning the day Pearson arrived to start
work—as he quips, blackly, "they waited for me")
and led to the next hospital scheme, this time via
Gray's recommendation: "Without lifting a
promotional finger I was called to Lagos and offered
the commission."[18]

A second large teaching establishment, the
University Teaching Hospital, Ilorin in Kwara State,
Nigeria had a similar programmatic requirement
to Damascus, the final 1977 brief from the Federal
Ministry of Health calling for a 500 bed hospital

ILORIN

Ilorin is at 8°30' N about 250 kilometres north of Lagos at an elevation of 360 metres, located north of the rain forest on the savannah grass land which is slightly undulating but relatively flat. The climate has high relative humidity, frequent sunshine and a rainy season.

Ilorin has a rainy season which lasts from April to October, with a maximum rainfall of about 200 mm in September. Minimum rainfall in December is about 8 mm.

Yearly average temperatures range from 38° C to 12° C. Unlike the rain forest where low cloud obscures the sun outside the rainy season, Ilorin has sunshine most of the time.

Relative humidity has a maximum monthly average of 91 per cent during September and October and a minimum monthly average of 77 per cent in February. Annual averages are 86 per cent maximum at 6.30 am and 55 per cent at 12.30 pm. The combination of temperature and humidity causes perspiration on the surface of the skin, which leads to severe discomfort. A strong flow of air across the body allows perspiration to evaporate and evaporative cooling improves comfort conditions.

The prevailing wind direction is from the southwest. When there is rain accompanied by wind protection of buildings against driving rain is necessary. Towards the end of the year the Harmattan wind blows from the northeast bearing dust, sometimes with low visibility.

Air temperature normally near to skin temperature, bodily heat loss to the air by convection or conduction is almost nil. There is also no significant cooling down at nights. Planning along east west axes, provides the best exposure to prevailing winds. With low rise buildings, widely spaced, wind shadows behind buildings can be minimised. Gaps between units and open corners of buildings encourage a venturi effect increasing pressure and also the air speed.

Roofs are pitched to shed water and concrete prevents rain noise on other materials. External walls set back from the exterior of buildings are of low thermal capacity allowing them to lose heat quickly. Habitable rooms are placed between two external balconies. One provides primary circulation and the other is a secondary route. Along these routes are vertical ducts open to the exterior but protected by metal work in local patterns. Horizontal pipes are suspended from balconies. This enables frequent spraying of the pipes with disinfectants and insecticides.

Windows are designed to allow maximum air circulation at body level. Hot air can escape through high level ventilation. To prevent dust due to Harmattan all windows can be closed. North and south facing windows have large openings, usually 40 to 80 per cent of wall areas.

Materials and construction techniques are selected for long span, speed of erection and ease of maintenance within the budget discipline of low cost building. Local materials are used and imported materials avoided where possible.

Except where air conditioning is required, rooms have ceiling fans to assist air movement.

Michael Pearson

(expandable to 1,000 beds once sufficient staff had been trained), a nursing school and staff accommodation. Here the Ministry's chief architect had determined broad principles, including low-rise buildings, compartmentalisation of departments to reduce the impact of power failure and limited air conditioning, familiar to Pearson from Damascus. However, in a country with very different climatic conditions and a lower level of available funds (Kwara was actually a less wealthy State even than others within Nigeria), Pearson tailored his detailed response accordingly.

Consideration of local particularities began with the very ground itself. Realising that the flattest part of the site—its summit—was the best location for building but was too small, and establishing that levelling works would be too costly, Pearson positioned the industrial zone on the hillside just below. Other facilities could then be erected on top, effectively extending the flat surface at no cost.

A grid was formed by wards, departments and connecting corridors. To minimise risk to patients (and service runs), operating theatres were placed adjacent to intensive care suites and surgical wards. As at Damascus, staff and visitors were separated.

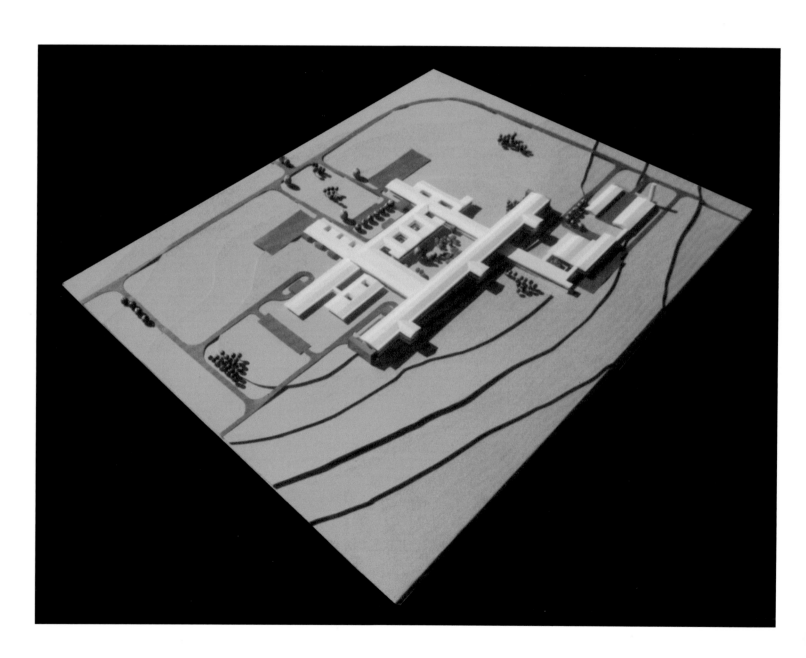

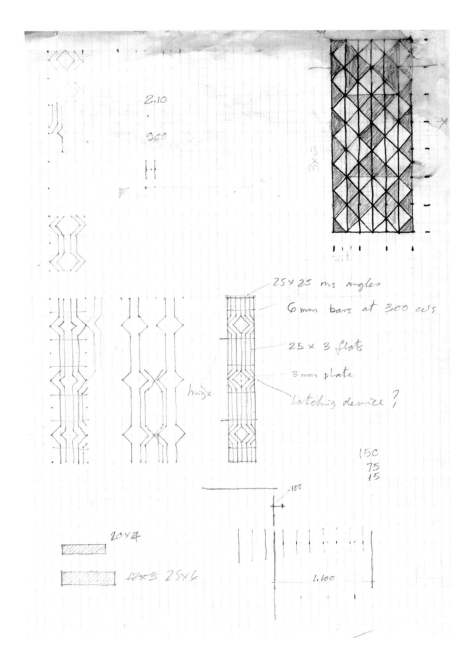

Opposite
Study model of the scheme with the grid layout of the component wings clearly visible, as well as details of site topography.

Above
Original sketch sheet, with notations by Pearson, showing the evolution of the Islamic design-inspired duct cover grilles.

In programming the hospital services, vertical ducts were accessed from corridors and balconies rather than rooms so that "the departmental space is not interrupted but merely served", an explicit reference to Kahnian theory that marks Pearson's increasing confidence.[19] The operating theatres—the most 'served' of all the spaces in a hospital—had two separate air conditioning units for redundancy to address the very high humidity and minimal variation in temperature throughout a 24 hour period that were the specific environmental problems at Ilorin. However, these were the only parts of the building to be artificially cooled because "anything mechanical [...] which stopped stayed that way. Except for electric fans which are widely used. Air conditioning unit[s] and windows which close are for the affluent."[20]

This ability to plan within the capacity of local infrastructure, having developed a detailed understanding of cultural, climatic and capability norms, was becoming a key differentiator: "When the scheme was [originally] submitted it was a high technology, air conditioned hospital suitable for Florida, the home state of the architect and engineers [...] But of course they hadn't a clue about Africa."[21]

For the remainder of the complex, Pearson turned instead to ways of encouraging the air movement across the skin and consequent evaporation that is the natural mechanism of cooling in such a climate. As a first step, buildings were located on the part of the site favoured by wind, again aligned east–west, and placed at the core of their blocks. Then:

> Rooms must be open to each side of a building. Wide balconies and overhanging roofs set above the top ceiling minimise solar gain and create a vortex of wind through a building and roof space. Courtyards must be as big as practicable to allow the wind to reassemble before hitting the next building. Corners of buildings are open to increase the flow.[22]

Perforations in the concrete balustrades contributed to the air movement. Many of these principles had been used by Jean Prouvé for his pre-fabricated tropical house design, which Pearson greatly admires as "superb [...] a fabulous piece of work, a fabulous concept".[23]

For amenity, an important factor in patient care, existing planting was to have been retained across the site with additional planting in the wind shadow areas of the courtyards, as with Damascus. This was intended to give "an awareness of the exterior in a deep building".[24] The decision not to level the site summit also led to trees and shrubs being retained.

The planning grid was a sub-division of the structural grid, allowing for the usual adaptability. The horizontal layout gave room for expansion, "without

Right
Artist's impression of
the completed buildings.
The wide external corridor-
balconies are prominent.

Opposite top
First floor plan.

Opposite bottom
Ground floor plan: both
showing the spread over a
wide area to minimise wind
shadows between buildings and
the relationship of disciplines.

disturbing the basic planning logic of inter-departmental relationships".[25] Within ward blocks, large-span bays interspersed with the fixed lift cores permitted a variety of spaces to be fashioned from non-load-bearing partitions, allowing sub-division or amalgamation as organisational change occurred. In the industrial zone, space was provided for extra kitchen and boiler plant to be installed should expansion occur; as may be recalled, Charles B and Charles E did this at Llandudno. Inherent was the ability to vary, merge or otherwise alter movement of users through the hospital if needed through changes to the spacing, size of and connections between corridors. This included the possibility of sales booths being installed in corridors if required.

In reducing capital and running costs as far as was compatible with the brief, ramps were used rather than lifts in many areas. The wide external corridors would have assisted regular and emergency access and protected the walls against the driving rain which is another feature of the region; one system therefore fulfilled several functions. Water, oil and sewage were gravity-fed to eliminate breakdown-prone pumps and condensate was to be returned to boilers for efficiency.

Writing on resource planning for hospital provision in Africa, Gray declared "a professional responsibility to present [...] clients with economic feasibility studies which examine not only questions of capital cost but those of recurrent cost, which must include proposed staffing patterns, geared to socio-economic assessments."[26]

Finally, a small but delightful example of Pearson's real sensitivity to the locale came in the prosaic form of the covers for the service ducts. To allow the ducts to be easily cleaned and sprayed with disinfectant the covers were in fact open grilles, but Pearson designed them in a pattern recalling the geometric designs characteristic of Islam, the predominant local religion in Kwara State.

Again, Ilorin progressed no further than completing documents ready for seeking tenders but even this allowed Pearson to test himself. Though original schemes resulted, in his use of low-rise, flexible space, separated but interrelated circulation and non-disruptive servicing it is hard not to see traces of contemporary British examples, especially the rigorously planned and highly mechanised Greenwich District Hospital of 1965–1974 for which Goodman was design team leader and, by its completion, chief architect of the Department.[27]

Pearson's and Gray's third hospital, in a third country, put them in a very different position, however. Damascus' plan was entirely within Pearson's control; Ilorin's had already been determined in principle but Pearson had some flexibility within this. At the Seth PD Hinduja Hospital, Bombay, India, not only had the design been agreed but construction had already started by the time he became involved in 1980.

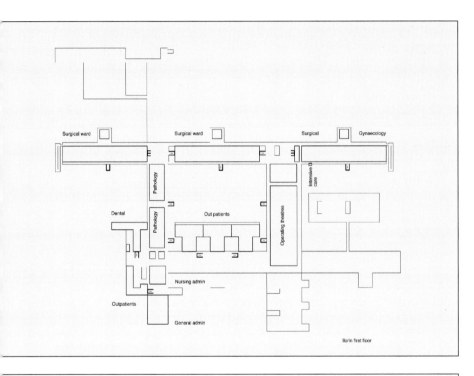

Ilorin first floor

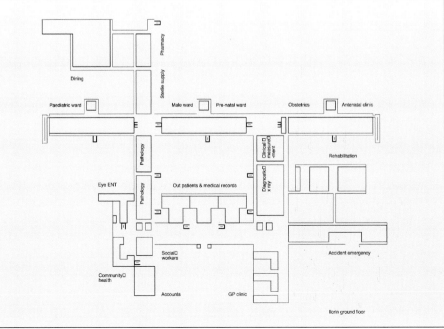

Ilorin ground floor

Indian architects IM Kadri had been commissioned to construct a 17-storey building for the expansion of the charitable hospital founded by philanthropist and businessman Shri Parmanand Deepchand Hinduja in 1951, with Shanning International providing hospital planning and equipping services. Above a rectilinear five-storey podium the remaining 12 floors, mostly wards, were designed to a pinwheel plan with additional projections for staircases, the whole being rotated 45 degrees with respect to the podium. The concrete structure had risen beyond the top of the latter when Pearson was subcontracted with Gray to support Shanning.

The pair's main focus was on planning the internal spaces, including provision for mechanical services, and developing related operational policies, but in doing so they found that "each of the projecting wings of the cruciform shape of the tower was not big enough, even two of them were not big enough, to really accommodate an economic ward size".[28]

Pearson compares the task to converting an old building, such was the difficulty. The work required the re-routing of services whose installation had already been designed; fortunately, Pearson was able to liaise with the engineering team and ensure that changes were made "just in time to avoid alterations to built fabric".[29]

A larger problem was the placement of the lifts. Whilst patients and visitors were provided with three lifts each in a central core, for social reasons doctors and nurses each had a single lift some distance away from these and from each other. The likely problem was obvious, but though raised by Pearson as a solvable problem even at this stage — "I told the senior brother that they should take the concrete down and re-locate the lifts" — no action was taken; when the hospital finally opened in 1986, staff experienced average lift waiting times of 20 minutes.[30] Revisiting ten vcharge that "they'd had every vertical transportation

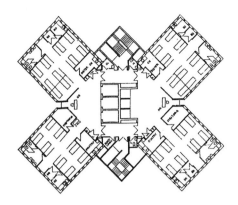

consultant in the world to have a look at it, and they can't find a solution".[31]

Bombay would seem to validate Pearson's and Gray's poor opinion of towers for adaptability and efficiency, and for hospitals in general; Pearson opines that the architect "thought he was building a 1950s Holiday Inn".[32]

Two private schemes provide a foil to Pearson's public work in this field.

An extension to the Corniche Maternity Hospital in Abu Dhabi, United Arab Emirates, was to be created in 1979 by a team led by Joannou and Paraskevaides of Nicosia, with Pearson. The extension was to contain, inter alia, a wing for the exclusive use of the Abu Dhabi Royal family. Vehicles would drive into a secure internal covered courtyard deep within the hospital, from where a lift and stair led to a dedicated, self-contained suite on the first floor containing a small ward, delivery room, kitchen and staff facilities. Rooms for guards were also provided, including sleeping quarters. Fully air conditioned, services were still supplied vertically and from small, stand-alone units to ease maintenance.

From a hospital with a private (very private) wing to one which was completely so; in 1981 healthcare group American Medical International proposed a hospital in Alexandria, Egypt for the city University's faculty staff to practice at privately. Pearson was part of the project team, and heartily embraced the differences in the brief as compared to Damascus and Ilorin. He created a concept whereby patient rooms "had the quality and image of an hotel", accessed by lift directly from the street and separated from the diagnosis and treatment rooms by a single "discreet" door on each floor, the only indication of their presence.[33] The building was air conditioned throughout and included other complex services — intriguingly, its external lift and stair cores and overall massing recalled Kahn's Alfred Newton Richards Medical Research Building — but Pearson

pposite bottom
he Hinduja hospital extension
ith bridge to the original
ospital building.

pposite top
lan of a typical floor of the
linduja hospital.

bove
rtist's impression of the
ecure Royal courtyard within
he extension to the Corniche
Maternity Hospital, Abu Dhabi.

still incorporated architectural features to minimise
heat build-up and aid natural cooling, such as walls
with high thermal mass and small windows within
deep moulded hoods. The latter was inspired by
the balconies of traditional houses Pearson had
seen whilst in Damascus, where "you can open
the windows and you can open the louvres and you
get different types of conditioning".[34]

    These unusual jobs where funding was much freer
shows the ease with which Pearson worked along all
points of a broad economic and client spectrum, whilst
maintaining control over the specifics of the hospital as
a building type and incorporating his personal tenets.

Commercial developments

Exposure to a fresh, international clientele also brought
the chance to design commercial buildings for the first
time, a very different type in some ways but one to which
the familiar Pearson principles were just as well suited.

    In late 1973, Charles B Pearson Son & Partners
was one of several firms to respond to a request from
developers Ebraham and Abdul Latif Eshaq for a mixed-
use retail, residential and commercial centre for Manama,
Bahrain on a site adjoining their Hilton Hotel, then
under construction in the capital. There was considerable

latitude in fulfilling the brief, but flexibility of use
for the space provided was stressed, to enable the
brothers to respond to market conditions by adjusting
the balance between elements, as was the need for
costs to be held to a minimum, albeit commensurate
with the specification.

    Pearson's longstanding interests in current
and future adaptability, close engagement with the
client and ever-present efforts to keep running costs
low had a clear resonance with this brief, though
here the latter was maximising income rather than
minimising expenditure.

    Once again treading carefully between the
client's wish for a tower "just for the iconic value"
and the proven practicality, adaptability and lesser
cost of low-rise buildings, Pearson's initial submission
was delivered — by Roland Paoletti — in February 1974.[35]

    The proposed main building was striking; a
long, narrow, mid-rise block bent to describe an 80
degree curve in plan and stepping down from nine
to four storeys, south to north. Pearson described
it, with some justification, as "an exciting and
unusual building form with great elegance".[36] The
exterior would feature repeated modular pre-cast
concrete units and balconies for shading. Housing

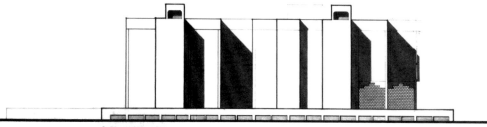

SIDE ELEVATION

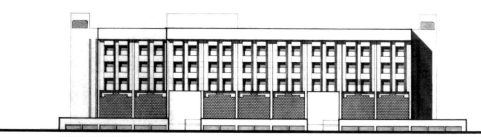

FRONT ELEVATION

the apartment and office units and some retail, the building was to be linked to the main double-height shopping mall which would have "the quality of the traditional Souk"; Bahrain has one of the more prominent permanent souks in the Gulf, and the linear nature of the main 'street' within the development would echo the typical layout of such bazaars.[37]

Within this envelope, the commercial elements were shown as being capable of change, either initially in the planning stage or subsequently in operation (and sometimes both). Shop units could be combined or kept separate, responding to shopping patterns as they develop; upper floors were to contain either flats or offices, the proportion of which could be altered according to demand; and these spaces could themselves be of varying size.

Following discussions with the Eshaqs, who commented on the economics of the proposal in light of current trends, additional flexibility was included such that the flats could, as a planning decision, have their living areas placed on the exterior, for views, or interior, for shade, as at Ilorin.

Other aspects, from foundation type to structural frame material to parking provision, were thoroughly re-considered for cost but without compromising the integrity of the architecture. Thus the higher end of the building was "below the height where building costs increase disproportionately", the costs of constructing the curved section were deemed "not significant" in comparison to "the advantage of this building form in the overall design" and even the stepped roofline "would not increase the cost since the total extent of gable end wall would be the same as for a building of constant height".[38]

Unsurprisingly, services were also re-considered. Mostly distributed vertically, they were placed "outside the useable floor area, on the exterior of the building in the balcony zone. The soil, waste, vents and water supply mains located here would be sized to accommodate the maximum future requirements of the building."[39]

This arrangement also permitted open or cellular division of that useable floor area.

Phased construction of the whole building was suggested, and given the clients' original wishes, additional stages designed as towers were incorporated into the overall plan if these became economically justifiable.

Pearson was keen to explore alternative environmental control technology on this project. Inspired by observation of Bahrain airport's buildings, Pearson mooted a metal cladding system to combat heat build-up. This, he felt, might also be "extremely attractive in creating an elegant and sophisticated building quite different from those in Manama at present" and could provide "the image of prestige which I feel that Messrs. Eshaq are looking for".[40] Pearson of course referenced Burne House as an illustration of the firm's technical expertise in

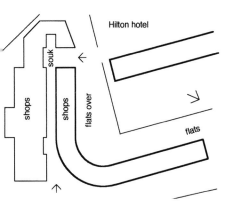

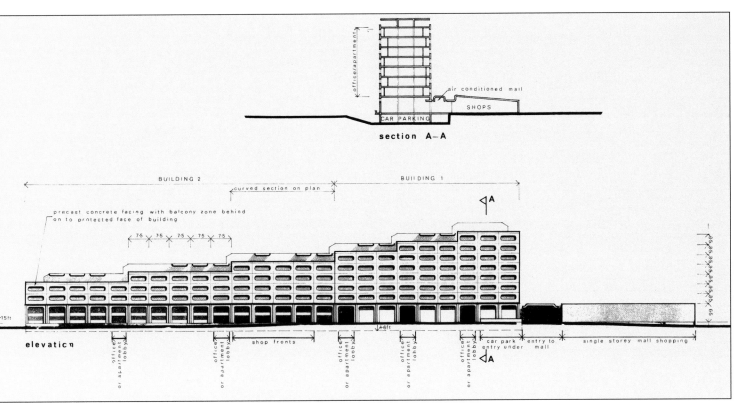

section A–A

BUILDING 2   curved section on plan   BUILDING 1

precast concrete facing with balcony zone behind on to protected face of building

elevation

this area. He also advocated a solar-assisted system suggested by engineers Ove Arup & Partners in which heat from the sun vaporises ammonia which subsequently condenses and cools, chilling the water used in the air conditioning. This conserves energy, reduces costs, is quieter in operation and reduces fossil fuel consumption. Recalls Pearson: "We were using heat exchangers on the roof to create chilled air for air conditioning. I mean this was something I was working on—fuel efficiency, natural conditioning schemes—30 years ago, never mind just now, when everybody's got so very excited about it."[41]

Though not a tower, Pearson's Bahrain building was still a leader of the now-widespread trend for memorable, visually arresting Gulf state buildings.[42]

Although its arc plan had clear antecedents in, for example, Morris Lapidus' dazzling, curved resort hotels, such as the Fontainebleau, Miami Beach, Florida of 1954, Pearson created an original, attractive commercial building which was well adapted to its locale and brief.

Five years later, Pearson designed a similar commercial centre in Amman, Jordan, this time comprising a multi-storey car park, offices and retail. The plot was awkward, not only sloping steeply to give a difference in level of around six floors across the site but also with the streets defining the two principal site boundaries themselves sloping in opposite directions due to their being part of a hairpin road climbing the hill. Pearson, though, was able to turn this into an advantage.

Wrapping floors of car parking and shops around
a tall rectangular tower of offices whose circulation
core served the entire development, he placed the small
shop units below the car parking levels on the lower,
north side of the site but reversed this arrangement
on the higher southern side. In this way pedestrians
had easy access to both sets of shops from the street.
A much larger retail unit, configurable as one department
store, two supermarkets or a supermarket and a chain
store, was placed below ground at the high side of the
site, reachable via the small shops along both edges
of the site (using the circulation core in the case of those
on the southern boundary).

The smaller units, which related in size to
existing shops, could be changed by consolidation or
division and some had an upper level which could
be brought into use by tenants if needed with the
insertion of a staircase. The tower floors were serviced
as offices or flats and could also be re-sized. The top

of the tower could be fitted out as a restaurant or club
and had a terrace.

Environmentally, some of the shops were protected
from solar gain by their position under the car park and
the tower's windows mostly faced north–south, with
brises soleil on the south facade created by extending
the floor slab beyond the window line on each storey.

The Amman job was designed and tendered for with
Tarmac International in just six weeks, and was planned
for fast erection. This speed and efficiency was something
Pearson increasingly stressed in his tenders for
international work, showing how rapidly he adapted to
the conditions in this new operational sphere. This may
on occasion have had implications for aesthetics — of
Amman, Pearson jokes that he "can't say it was
architecture", and its elevations do possess a utilitarian
quality — but the quality of spacial manipulation in
response to site topography demonstrated by Pearson
in both featured projects belies the speed of design, and

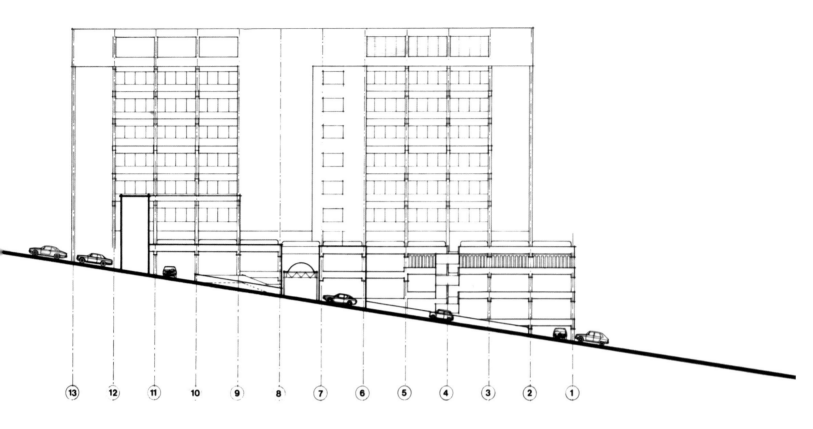

at Jordan, especially, harks back to Burne House and even Lancaster Royal Grammar School in its adroitness.[43]

Competitions

All of the foregoing came to Pearson through commission or submission, but interwoven with these, and begun whilst he was still working in Britain, were a trio of dynamic, imaginative competition entries that bring to light yet another aspect of Pearson's work through the unique nature of the competition as a generative medium.

Since a competition omits the iterative discussion and amendment which so typify Pearson's working method, reviewing these allows insight into designs which are certainly complete but which are also frozen in time, at the point just prior to the client's first reaction. They thus represent a chance to see Pearson proposals before the power of process is extended to the user, and to judge them accordingly.

Additionally, the surroundings within which Pearson was operating changed once more since the schemes selected for this chapter were to be built in continental Europe and include his ideas for two of the most publicised and prestigious architectural contests of recent years.

Finally, of course, competition entries ensured Pearson remained on the continuum begun by his grandfather and maintained by his father, and on

which he himself had first alighted with the Ashton Crown Local Office.

In 1969, French president Georges Pompidou announced a desire for a contemporary arts centre with elements of museum and production based on a two hectare (c. five acre), long-vacant site in the somewhat rundown Beaubourg district of Paris. Within two years a formal competition was launched with a broad set of criteria around intellectual accessibility. Although a revival of national art was intended, a positive local effect was undoubtedly hoped for also. Relevant, too, is that Paris was already mired in one controversial urban regeneration plan— removal of the produce market of nearby Les Halles to the suburbs, with demolition of its much-admired nineteenth century iron pavilions.

Pearson's entry into the Centre Pompidou competition was a vast but simple lattice steel box; a much-enlarged version of his Crown Local Office concept, in essence. However, the increased size prohibited the use of trusses alone to support the roof, so cables ran to six lattice towers placed within the building's footprint—the only interruptions to its open plan. This was filled with facilities including performance spaces, tiered seating, museums and galleries for permanent and temporary use, a cafe and a restaurant. In the true spirit of the times, areas of 'free space' were also provided. A library and vehicle parking

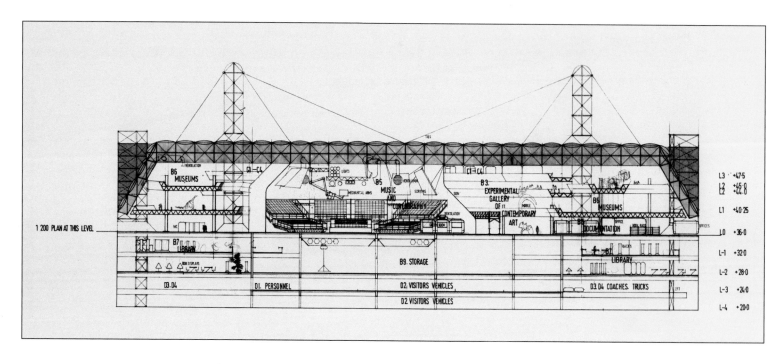

Above and opposite
Pompidou Centre competition
entry cross section and plan.

lay below ground, and air conditioning and lighting rigs
were mounted within the roof structure.

Surviving drawings indicate a fabric, or inflated
'cushion' covering, of the sort employed by Nicholas
Grimshaw at the Eden Project, Cornwall in 2001, for
the roof. Asked for more details of what was intended,
Pearson disarmingly admits that "I don't think we
even considered it", confirming competition entries as
the home of thought-through but still outline designs.[44]
In fact, Pearson's detailed research into inflatable
enclosures carried out in 1967 would certainly account
for such a finish, even before the invention of the
ethylene tetrafluoroethylene (ETFE) plastic used
at Cornwall.[45]

Pearson's was one of a staggering 680 entries.
Remarkably, the nine member jury was chaired by
Jean Prouvé, although his contact with Pearson in
1970 did not, it seems, sway his mind, and the winners
were announced as Richard Rogers, Renzo Piano and

Gianfranco Franchini, assisted by Ove Arup & Partners.[46]
Their entry had similarities to Pearson's, but its proposals
for a building of external walkways, roof-mounted
cranes and (re-)moveable features containing news, art,
television, robots, projections and an 'information wall'
were much closer to Archigram or Cedric Price's 1964 Fun
Palace. Its solid, translucent or glazed cladding panels,
open structure and, originally, Prouvé-style portholes did,
though, speak the same language as Pearson's Crown
Local Office and then-nascent design for Burne House.

A few years later, in 1977, Austrian authorities
announced a competition to design an extension
of the government quarter in Vienna on a site
between Ballhausplatz and Minoritenplazt near
the Volksgarten. Pearson designed an irregular
quadrilateral building for the space with windows
punched deeply into plain facades. The heart of
the scheme, however, was an internal courtyard
covered with a translucent gridshell.

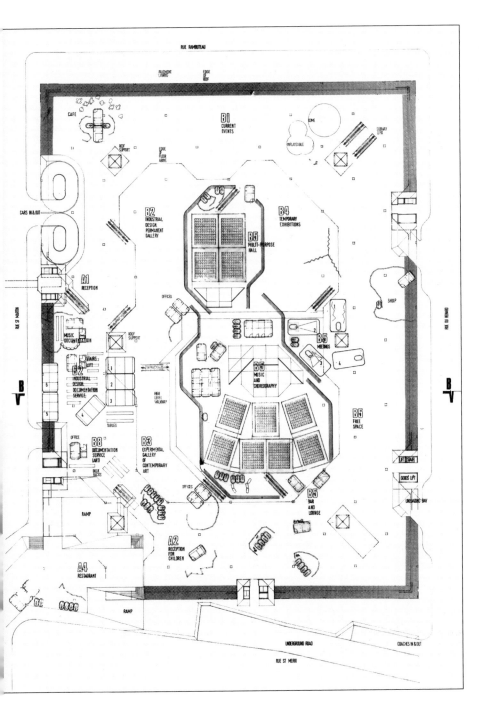

A gridshell is a structure of double curvature form, as with the surface of an egg or a balloon, usually built flat and deformed into its final shape. Pearson envisaged "a central six sided dome joined to the surrounding [walls] by side shells" with additional support from below at those joints.[47] Pearson had explored the idea the year before with his competition entry for new National Assembly Buildings in Abu Dhabi, United Arab Emirates; a gridshell dome evoked Islamic architecture and used louvres to exclude the sun in a system designed by Ian Liddell of Buro Happold, and Liddell created the roof for Pearson's Vienna scheme as well.[48]

It is apparent Pearson was aware of new developments which were in any case in line with his own thinking and research, and was including them in his designs as appropriate.

A decade after the Pompidou a second Parisian competition, inspired by a new president, saw Pearson put forward a brilliantly original example of lateral thinking which also took his occasional fondness for whimsy to a new height—quite literally.

The aim of the 1982 Tête Défense competition—one of new president François Mitterand's original grand projects—was to create an 'International Communications Crossroads', house ministerial offices and beget a monument to mark the two hundredth anniversary of the French Revolution in 1989, all at the western end of l'axe historique, the near eight kilometre (c. four mile) linear alignment of streets and structures that runs from the Louvre, through the Arc de Triomphe and out to the post-war La Défense district where almost all of Paris' skyscrapers are clustered.

For the competitors—over 400 of them—there appeared an obvious question, which had plagued attempts to build here since 1973: should the new edifice close the axis, or leave it open? Was the answer a building, like those on the surrounding esplanade,

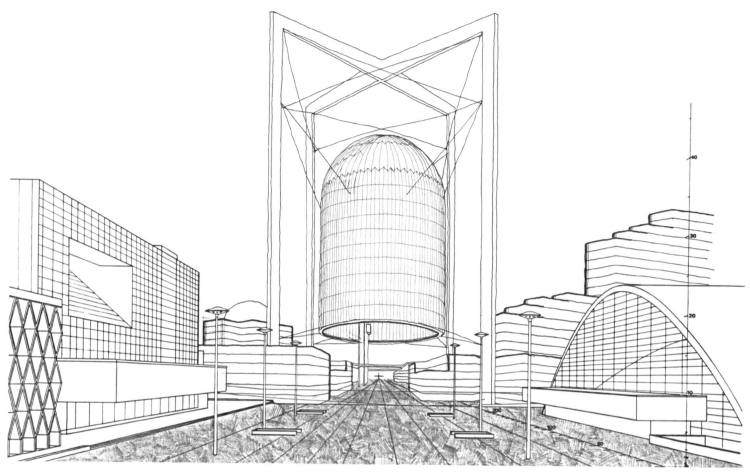

or a structure, like the Tour Eiffel, which was also a commemorative piece? The competition brief attempted clarification: "it is a matter of ending a layout inherited from the past and of announcing a plan orientated to the future[, ending] one perspective view and open[ing] up another".[49]

Pearson's reply was simple and ingenious and addressed both perceived alternatives in one design, as well as the topography of l'axe (mentioned in the brief) which causes only structures over a certain height to be visible under the Arc de Triomphe when seen by an observer in the Place de la Concorde.

He proposed "a visual image on the axis which one can see through or past" when approaching Paris from the northwest along the A14 motorway, preserving views of the Arc de Triomphe beyond.[50] Pearson actualised this image in glass as a large cylindrical volume capped with a dome whose proportions were actually derived from Jean-François Chalgrin's Arc de Triomphe, specifically "the rounded arch within it, rotated" about its vertical axis.[51]

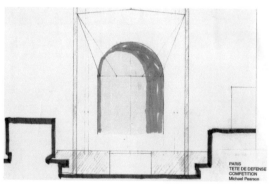

Pearson thus took a negative space and from it created a positive architectural volume which would be visible by day and illuminated at night. In an echo of the Centre Pompidou it would also be a screen for projected images and a base for communications equipment, and so again Archigram comes to mind. Its height—around 100 metres—was such that it "would have become visible the nearer you got [when approaching from central Paris;] it would start to rise up over the horizon".[52]

The dome and cylinder were to be realised practically as a framework of steel suspended by cables from four large columns and clad with toughened glass panels. Glazed lifts within would lead to observation galleries; maintenance access was through lifts and stairs inside the columns.

The office accommodation was placed around this centrepiece in buildings stepped in profile "so that people could sit on the balconies and look at films or whatever on the cylinder".[53] These buildings were to be finished in "a smooth skin of glass and vitreous enamel sheet steel panels connected with gaskets and bolted, from behind, to a metal framework spanning between floor slabs [giving] a clean appearance".[54]

The borrowing from Burne House is obvious and was not limited to the visual. The structural and planning grid were intended for maximum flexibility, air conditioning was to be a mixture of centrally chilled water and locally handled air and service runs were to be co-located with other fixed elements and have short, easily-changed runs of ducting. Even Pearson's and Allford's discussion of brises soleil returned, the entry document stating that "Projecting, non-ferrous metal louvres will be explored and developed as a sun shading system"—albeit this time firmly restricted to "all windows exposed to solar gain".[55]

The competition winner was Danish architect Johan Otto von Spreckelsen's Grand Arche de La Défense, an immense open white marble-clad cube which mixed the symbolic and the functional as requested (offices are contained within its base, walls and roof) and which has duly become one of Paris' landmarks, albeit not one universally loved. The brief's concept of the visitor having "access to events all over the world [...] through a host of media brought together daily" must have appeared rather quaint even before the rise of the internet made erecting a building for this purpose unnecessary, and today it is tired-looking and often quiet.[56]

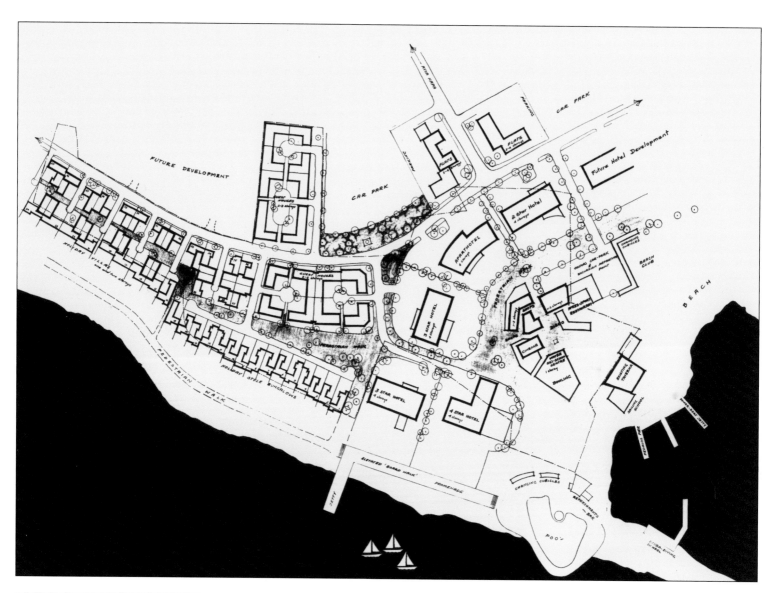

Top
Agia Napa, 1973–1975
The masterplan of this leisure
complex included villas, guest
houses, bungalows and hotels,
as well as a marina.

Bottom
National Iranian Oil Company
hospital, Ahwaz, Iran, 1976
Two ward blocks were linked to a
central diagnostic and treatment
block in this private company
hospital; deep, complex facade
articulation provides shade.

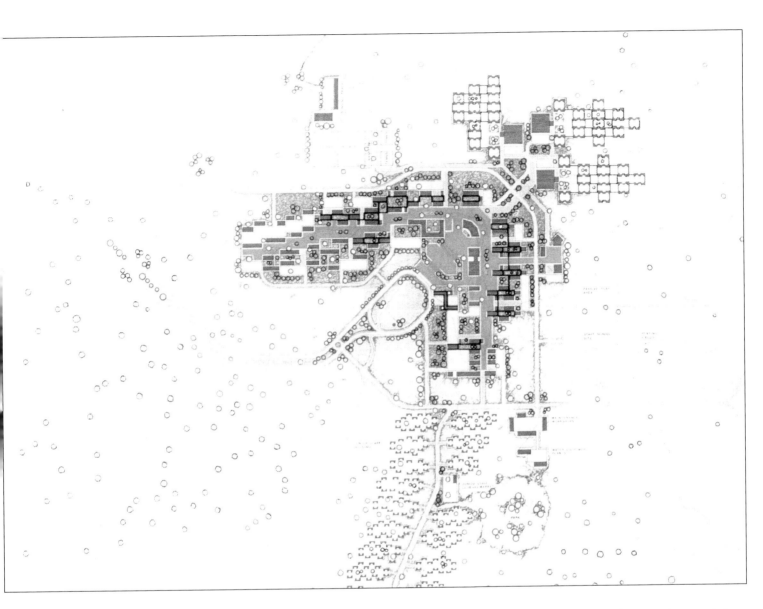

Above
Federal, Makurdi, Nigeria,
1981–1983.
Topography and climate informed
the placement of a campus of
four adaptable, expandable
colleges around a central street
cranked at communal buildings,
with perimeter servicing. Design
included a college of agriculture
with demonstration enterprises
on site, including for large
animals. Overall campus size
was around 4,800 hectares.

Pearson believes it shares a simple theme with other grand projects, namely "geometric simplicity; [...] the library is a flat platform [...] with four L-shaped books at the corners, the Tête Défense was two standard slab blocks with a top over it [and] at the Bastille, the opera [house is] virtually a cylinder, seen from the road".[57]

With this in mind, it is worth considering critic Andrew Ayres' note that some feel it "supremely ironic that a monument to the twentieth century should consist of a gigantic void".[58]

In light of such views, it is fascinating to speculate on how Pearson's intelligent inversion, simultaneously presence and absence, would have fared had it been built.

Other works abroad

Pearson's keenness for immersing himself in new, stretching ("It was extraordinary. I don't know whether it was tiring; we used to work on aeroplanes, and all sorts of tables") but invigorating environments that will drive his architecture forward yet keep it fully consistent with his beliefs is obvious, as the examples of various projects illustrated in the remainder of this chapter testify.[59] The only question which remained was what to do when this period ended.

1   In October 1973 Egypt, Syria and Iraq launched a joint military operation during the Jewish Yom Kippur and Muslim Ramadan to re-take land which had been occupied by Israel during the Six Day War of 1967.

2   MP, "Week by Week", *Building Design*, 13 April 1979. Exchange control restrictions involved governments placing limits on transactions in foreign currencies to balance the amounts entering and leaving the country.

3   Ibid. When the Knights of the Order of St John were driven from Rhodes, they eventually established a new home on Malta. Following the epic Siege of Malta in 1565 the Order's Grand Master, Jean de la Valette, determined that a new, fortified city was required to protect the remaining Knights. The Pope's architect, Francesco Laparelli, was requested to assist. He arrived in Malta on 28 December 1565 and had plans for the new city, later Malta's capital, ready within three days.

4   MP, "Week by Week", *Building Design*.

5   MP, in conversation with the author, 12 February 2008.

6   MP, in conversation with the author, 29 February 2008.

7   Export Credits Guarantee Department; British government department which insures British exporters against non-payment by their overseas buyers, guarantees bank loans and assesses political risk; MP, in conversation with the author, 22 July 2008.

8   MP, email to the author, 21 July 2008.

9   Pearson actually calculated that patients could be evacuated in an emergency more quickly simply by being suspended in a blanket and conveyed down the stairs.

10 Interestingly, in light of Pearson's admiration of the speed of planning of Valletta, the brief for the Pentagon was issued on a Thursday and plans and a perspective were ready the following Monday, after what Lieutenant Colonel Hugh J Casey, co-designer of this initial scheme, called—with admirable understatement—"a very busy weekend".

11 Estimated as "the population of the Festival Hall disgorging after a performance" (MP, email to the author, 21 July 2008).

12 MP, In conversation with the author, 16 October 2007.

13 MP, in conversation with the author, 29 February 2008.

14 MP, in conversation with the author, 22 July 2008.

15 & 16 MP, letter to the author, 7 September 2007; MP, in conversation with the author, 22 July 2008.

17 Gray, David, "Damascus University Teaching Hospital", January 1979.

18 MP, in conversation with the author, undated; MP, email to the author, 21 July 2008.

19 Federal Ministry of Health and Social Welfare, Ilorin Teaching Hospital, Planning Report, July 1979.

20 MP, email to the author, 21 July 2008.

21 MP, in conversation with the author, 22 July 2008.

22 MP, email to the author, 21 July 2008.

23 MP, in conversation with the author, 12 February 2008.

24 & 25 Federal Ministry of Health and Social Welfare, Ilorin Teaching Hospital, Planning Report.

26 Gray, David, "Economics of hospital planning in Africa"—draft article for *African Health*, undated.

27 Greenwich used the 'Universal Hospital Structure', with services limited to the usual cores plus equipment-only sub-floors layered horizontally. This was thought to free more floor space than using vertical segregation. It used Vierendeel trusses to create both the column-free main floors and, by threading services through the trusses themselves, the service floors. Louis Kahn took the same approach at the Salk Institute, La Jolla, California, in 1959–1965. Greenwich was based on extensive analysis of personnel flows, work patterns and even movements of every type of supply. Air conditioning, automated conveyors, paternosters and escalators for visitors featured; in a telling contrast to Pearson's approaches, all of these systems either failed or required considerable maintenance to be kept operating, despite use in an advanced industrial nation. The hospital closed in 2001 and was demolished in 2005–2007.

28 MP, in conversation with the author, 11 July 2008.

29 *General hospital, Bombay, India*, Pearson Architects brochure, c. 2000.

30-32 MP, in conversation with the author, 22 July 2008.

33 Pearson Architects brochure, c. 1990.

34 MP, in conversation with the author, 16 September 2008.

35 MP, in conversation with the author, 22 July 2008.

36 & 37 "Proposed commercial and residential development

adjoining Bahrain Hilton Hotel site for Investment & Trading (Gulf) Enterprises", Charles B Pearson Son & Partners, February 1974.

38 & 39   "Proposed commercial and residential development adjoining Bahrain Hilton Hotel site for Investment & Trading (Gulf) Enterprises", Supplementary report, Charles B Pearson Son & Partners, March 1974.

40   MP, letter to RD Read, 5 May 1974.

41   MP, in conversation with the author, 15 February 2008.

42   Interestingly, Basil Spence's last design before his death, in 1976, was for an audaciously designed cultural centre for Bahrain mixing Western and Arab ideas.

43   MP in conversation with the author, 22 January 2008.

44   MP, in conversation with the author, 22 July 2008.

45   ETFE was developed in the 1970s as an insulation for the aircraft industry, but was only used in architecture from the 1980s.

46   Prouvé may have been attracted to the cast steel cantilevers or gerberettes in the Rogers scheme; Edmund Happold, co-founder of structural engineers Buro Happold, once told Pearson that, having been aware of the Rogers scheme, seen an atmospheric Parisian foundry of the kind which would be needed to produce them and knowing Prouvé's blacksmith background, he encouraged Rogers to emphasise the gerberettes in his presentation. However, Pearson notes that Happold "might have been pulling my leg" (MP, in conversation with the author, 11 July 2008).

47   Annotated competition entry image, undated.

48   Liddell later received a CBE for the engineering of the Millennium Dome, London. Pearson's National Assembly had cleverly separated routes for the public and assembly members and water features which also reflected Islamic tradition but acted as cooling units for the air conditioning as well. Happold had a long-term interest in lightweight, tensile structures including the architectural use of ETFE, and had worked with German architect and engineer Frei Otto on buildings such as the gridshell-based Mannheim Multihalle, completed only in 1975.

49   *Extract from the competition file, Tête Défense Concours international d'architecture*, Electa Moniteur, 1984.

50   Document supporting Pearson International's entry in the Tête Défense competition, Paris, October 1982.

51   MP, in conversation with the author, date unrecorded.

52   MP, in conversation with the author, 7 August 2008.

54 & 55   Tête Défense competition document.

56   *Extract from the competition file, Tête Défense Concours international d'architecture*; France's hugely successful pre-internet Minitel telephone-based information terminals were launched the same year as the Tête Défense competition.

57   MP, in conversation with the author, 7 August 2008. The references are to Dominique Perrault's Bibliothèque Nationale de France,1995, and Carlos Ott's Opéra Bastille, 1989, to which might be added Pei's pyramid at the Louvre,1989, and Adrien Fainsilber's spherical Géode IMAX cinema,1985.

58   Ayres, Andrew, *The Architecture of Paris, An Architectural Guide*, Edition Axel Menges, 2004.

59   MP, in conversation with the author, 22 July 2008.

British Works II

8

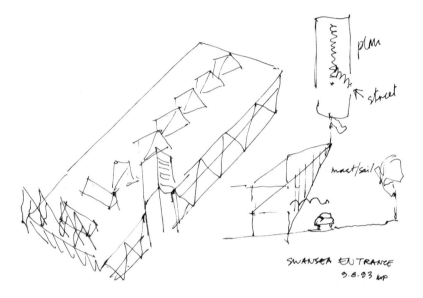

SWANSEA ENTRANCE
9.8.93 kmp

After a decade working almost exclusively abroad, Pearson returned to Britain in 1983 to what were lean years personally. He was buoyed initially by "an endless series of conversions of buildings into flats", a continuation of an aspect of his practice begun in the 1970s.[1]

The maintenance study of Burne House referred to in chapter six then led to a near 15 year relationship with BT's London operation. This work comprised building alterations for new apparatus, designs and improvements for offices (many undertaken as Pearson Interiors, a partnership of Pearson and his second wife), landscaping, surveys and maintenance. Beneficial in itself, it also freed Pearson to enter competitions and seek other commissions.

As in his early years of practice a mix of projects, built and unbuilt, resulted. This chapter highlights two for their variation on the Pearson process of iteration: a competition design's unfolding, with no reference to the client, can be witnessed through extensive pre-submission development sketches, whilst Fishergate is a rare example of enforced compromise which made Pearson distinctly unhappy.

A few years later, another chance meeting resulted in a sustained association with the South East Reserve Forces' and Cadets' Association (SERFCA), an agency of the Ministry of Defence, that continues to this day. Two of Pearson's strikingly stripped-down, economic, yet elegant accommodation buildings for this client, one for people and one for machines, are examined which take his old concerns into new areas and a new century.

Pearson also acted in many building defect and construction dispute cases, connecting straight back to one of his first professional jobs and often proving the importance of architect-user-client discussion at the outset of a scheme.

In 1993, competition entrants for a business centre in Swansea, at Penllergaer business park, were briefed to include both managed and lettable units and a conference area. Pearson saw the chance to revisit and "explore [...] the spatial and organisational potential of a deep plan, two-storey building, with a repeating simple structural bay, naturally ventilated and with daylighting mainly gained through the roofs".[2]

Visiting the site, Pearson immediately saw the potential of topography, including an existing earthen bank and the local road layout, to "give this building a little predominance over the rest" and create "a street building rather than an isolated pavilion" that would provide a "stop" for this end of the park.[3]

An absorbing sequence of sketches charts the evolution of the complete building plan from this simple starting point.

The centre was to be fully adaptable internally within the "game [...] rules defined by its fixed elements".[4] This translated into a lettable area able to be subdivided for multiple occupancy, partitioned as required within this and expanded into the remainder of the building if necessary, an optional suspended ceiling and a conference area capable not only of being reshaped as needed with sliding/folding doors but

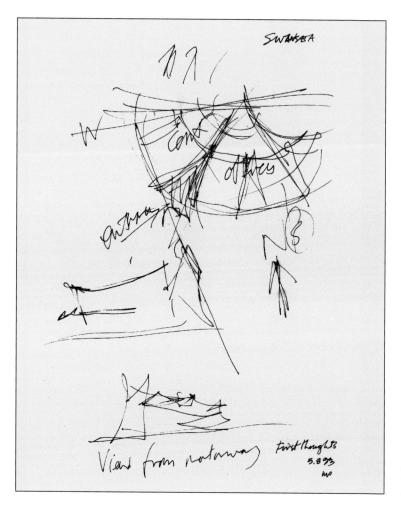

SWANSEA

View from motorway

First thoughts
5.8.93
MP

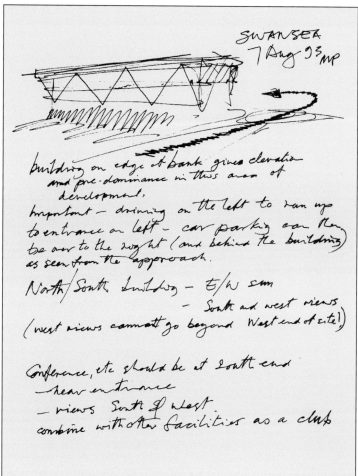

SWANSEA
7 Aug 93 MP

building on edge of bank gives elevation
and pre-dominance in this area of
development.
Important — driving on the left to run up
to entrance on left — car parking can then
be over to the right (and behind the building)
as seen from the approach.

North/South building — E/W sun
— South and west views
(west views cannot go beyond West end of site)

Conference, etc should be at South end
— near entrance
— views South & West.
combine with other facilities as a club

Opposite and previous page
The Swansea scheme emerged in just four days, as shown by these dated sheets. The site itself generates the entire plan; the placing, the approach, the swing round to the entrance – on the opposite side to preserve views – which in turn suggests a convex end to the block, and the acutely-angled 'cut' deep into that side for a lobby. The final sketch shows the roof north lights.

Right
Orientation, amenity, appearance, structure and environmental conditioning are captured on this one sheet of details; note use of Prouvé-like 'portal' frames, here with a double cantilever and before introduction of the lantern light above them.

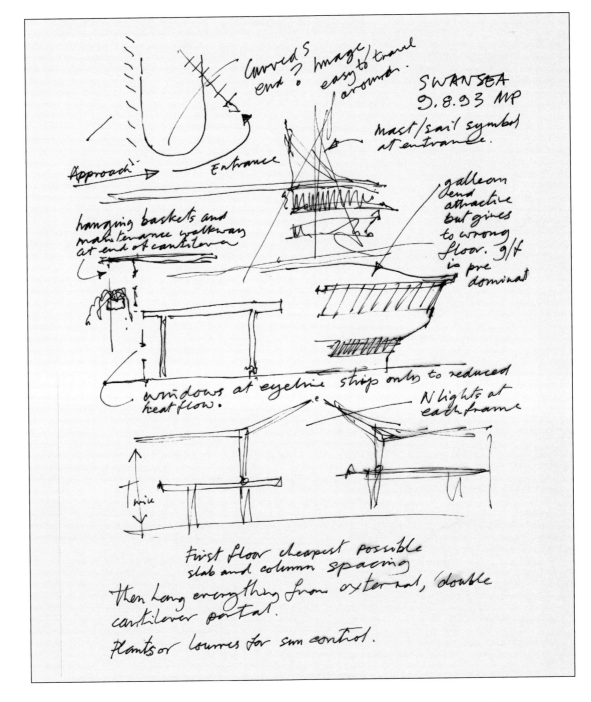

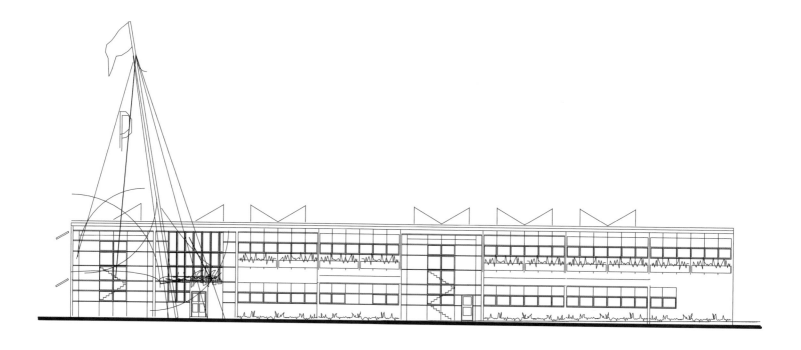

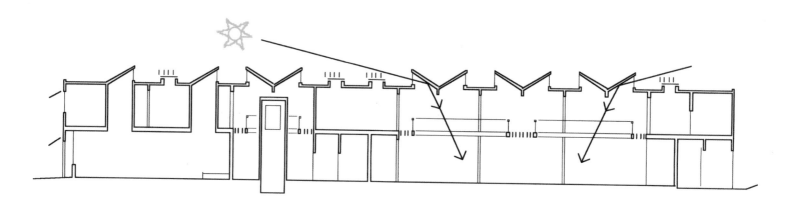

Top
Swansea: entrance
elevation.

Bottom
Sunlight controlled for
winter conditions.

also of being opened onto an outside terrace for overspill or vehicular access.

A steel and pre-cast concrete structure allowed a triple-height central atrium, driving natural ventilation via the stack or chimney effect. This minimised artificial conditioning, which was proposed to be energy-efficient and micro-controllable where installed. In a first for Pearson, which was to inform later work, canvas screens were to be installed to "direct light, to reflect light downwards or inwards from [the] central core".[5] Externally elevations were to be of stained timber, continuing Pearson's established feel for materials but now enabled by a recent fire regulation change (Pearson would return to this as well), with louvres and planters hung from the structure contributing to cooling.

This was the beginning of the wireless computing age, causing Pearson to scribble on one sketch "is this

the end of the raised floor?", doubtless also in response to his growing view that "cabling was becoming an impossible problem in some of these buildings", a view which he feels "started with Burne House...".[6]

The project also came in the middle of a recession. Flexibility would provide economic resilience, but Pearson saw this as a time where "as routine competence becomes easily available the need for creativity and human interaction will be paramount".[7] Swansea was therefore to feature a club with restaurant and bar which Pearson likened to his then practice base at 5 Dryden Street in Covent Garden, London, a working community of individual design firms built around communal facilities, and the more conventional bar at the AA. He envisaged something "like the bus station, where everyone passes, enabling casual contact", possibly also attracting workers from across the business park.[8]

op
outh elevation.

Middle and bottom
wansea cross-sections
how conditions.

Winter conditions
Day
lanting dormant, window blinds
pen, allow solar gains; windows
losed, trickle ventilators open;
rickle ventilators in centre
ooflights controlled by air
stack effect; perimeter panel
adiators with ventilators run
from condensing boiler at
variable flow and temperature
reduce gas consumption; high
insulation to roof, walls, floor
and glazing reduces heat loss;
high efficiency diffuser down
lighting, suspended at 2.6 metres
to reduce power consumption,
with effect up lighting to reduce
shadows and improve perceived
quality; canvas sail reflectors
direct natural light to lower floor.

Night
high insulation and closable
trickle ventilators reduce
heat loss; massive floor slab
attenuates heat loss and reduces
peak boiler capacity.

Summer conditions
Day
centre high level windows
open to allow day and night
ventilation; heat gains to south
facing rooflight blinds improve
stack effect ventilation; thermally
massive floor slabs absorb
internal heat gains; external
planting in full growth minimises
solar heat gains; separate
ventilation and glass for views
provide maximum use control;
north facing rooflights provide
natural illumination to centre
area; canvas sail reflectors direct
light to lower floor; light coloured
surfaces reflect light maximising
efficiency of sources.

Night
small, secure ventilators
left open to continue night
ventilation; excess heat
convected away; night air cooling
of slabs provides additional heat
absorption next day.

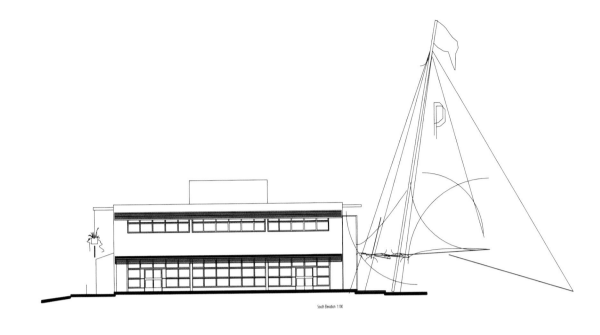

South Elevation 1:100

Winter

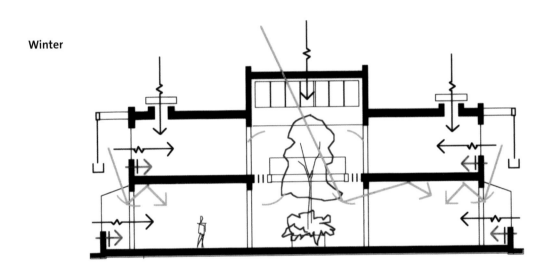

Summer

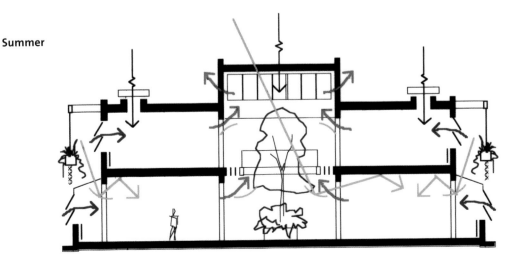

Top
Swansea: first floor plan.

Bottom
Swansea: ground floor plan.

Opposite
1   First floor, lettable
    space, as brief
2   First floor, possible
    smaller lettable space
3   First floor, extended
    lettable space
4   First floor, minimum
    lettable space
5   Ground floor,
    conference facilities,
    as brief
6   Ground floor, extended
    conference or exhibition
    facilities
7   Ground floor, more
    extended conference
    or exhibition facilities.

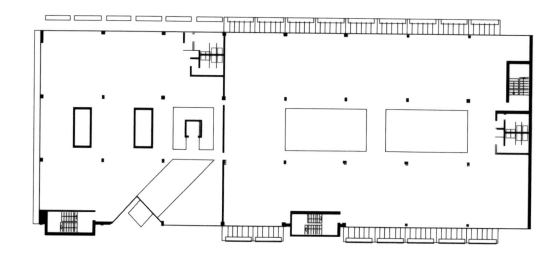

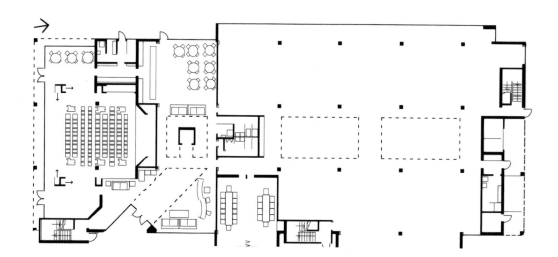

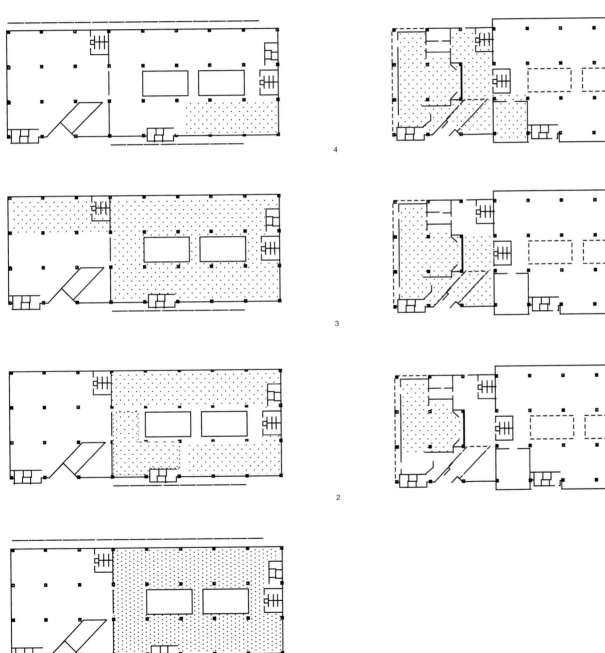

4

3

2

1

7

6

5

TV studio for broadcasting American football, working at speed from brief to completion in 14 weeks.

This rumination over how people interact and relate within a building furthers another of the threads running through Pearson's work, detectable at Lancaster Royal Grammar School, Mayford and the hospital schemes (Pearson's own preference for working in small, multi-skilled teams forms a strand of this thread). However, its application to new, developing ways of office employee working, with less rigorous patterns of movement and more informal spaces, is noteworthy. Intriguingly, Frank Duffy believes that analysis can predict what office space should be like, in contrast to Pearson's and Landau's theories.

Familiar in concept from his Crown Local Office designs, Swansea saw Pearson's principles updated but displaying fundamental relevance even after 30 years. An instinctive response to site, briskly efficient usage of space and expanded concern for economics produced a building which would have been a positively atypical addition to the business park. Unfortunately it remained unbuilt, but in many ways proved to be a useful indicator of the direction Pearson's architecture would move in subsequently.

Informed by his work abroad, such as the heat exchanger system at Bahrain, Pearson's buildings became crisper, leaner, cheaper to maintain and even more environmentally sustainable (this having been addressed by Pearson well before that label became commonplace).

Thus an unexecuted design for an adaptable arts centre for Leicester the same year was timber-clad and also timber-framed, and was naturally-lit and ventilated. Wonderfully, its facades also featured distinctive 'slot' windows, linking back directly to Lancaster Royal Grammar School 35 years previously.

Pearson also acted with yet greater speed to aid survival in this return of recessionary times, having warmed up in 1989 with a rapid (14 week) exercise to create—with Patrick Garnett, a fellow

Manchester student and later co-founder of Garnett Cloughley Blakemore & Associates—a television studio within a portion of a former Lyons restaurant which was originally the ballroom of the Trocadero music hall, just off Piccadilly Circus, London, in which "Negotiations and approvals were phased in parallel with the construction programme and just ahead of the contractor's works."[9]

Two years later, Pearson received a commission for a small residential and retail development in Norwich, on Fishergate, near the centre of the city.

On an infill plot close to the River Wensum, several compact two bedroom flats were to be erected above a new retail unit and surface parking. As at Swansea, Pearson saw that the location could be unlocked: "the magic about that site was that once you were on the first floor, every front pair of rooms looked straight at the cathedral" to the south east.[10] This was in tune with the brief, which supposed housing "for middle class people, children gone away, getting older, and it was so the bedroom could become the living room and [...] the [other] bedroom was next to [...] the kitchen, so there was close contact between the one who was in bed ill and the other one in the house".[11]

The adjacent buildings were of little architectural merit but were no higher than three storeys plus roof, and Pearson intended to address this context: "Well what I was trying to do was keep in reasonable scale with the buildings along the frontage and let the tower rise up at the back so it would be seen from a distance."[12]

The local conservation officer supported the idea of a tower, considering that "here was the place for another vertical interruption" in the skyline given various buildings of similar height beyond the immediate vicinity.[13]

In massing the lower levels, Pearson drew on the vernacular, by "stepping out, coming out horizontally over the previous storey, [...] a traditional technique in Norwich for the old Mediaeval buildings—they put the floor joists down and let them hang over a couple of feet".[14]

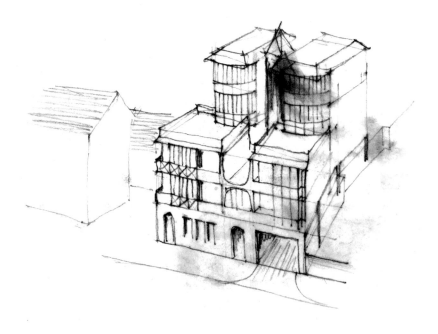

Two sketches depicting the original Fishergate scheme at Norwich, with 'skyline' tower above the three-storey base and contemporary finishes to both. Note the box balcony conservatories on the lower section.

The ensuing box-like projections were not simply for visual effect but were "absolutely crucial" to each flat's plan, utility and environmental conditioning, because—as at Alexandria—they were also informed by, and would function like, a traditional local precedent, on this occasion, the "Maltese traditional balcony, [which is] really an air conditioning box, it's where you hang your laundry to dry it when the sun's out and you can get it to take in cool air."[15]

The geometry of this box, augmented with a suitable divider, allowed two linked climatic zones to be formed. The outer zone, a balcony, would reflect exterior conditions, becoming cool, warm or hot according to the season, but the inner zone would buffer this, ameliorating the heat in summer whilst providing warmth in winter and ensuring a comfortable temperature. Moreover, the amenity of the cathedral views was preserved when seated quite deeply within the flat. Reference back to the second-iteration planning stage at Bahrain, regarding the placing of living areas, is instructive.

Pearson's effective combination of two very different architectural traditions—English and Maltese—is in line with other earlier works where apparently variant sources have been merged, such as Middleton's Kahnian plan and Lancashire vernacular finishes, Shackcliffe's Miesian steel and Smithsonian concrete and, of course, the Crown Local Offices.

Crucially, a contemporary look was intended for both elements of the block, with extensive glazing being applied to the boxed conservatories and bow windows in the tower. It was at this point, though, that conservation and restoration lobbies became concerned over the scheme, with suggestions of pantiles, pitched roofs and beaded panelling for the conservatory exteriors emerging.

Although Pearson had happily contextualised his building to a degree, and boundary walls would be carefully worked with reference to neighbouring materials and styles, he did not agree with this pastiche approach to the development as a whole. Pearson's client, however, was advised that planning permission would be more favourably considered and accordingly "he succumbed and I had to do his bidding".[16] Later a reduction in height ordered by other authorities, despite the indication given earlier, reduced the number of flats that could be included and thus made the entire concept uneconomic, causing its abandonment.

Pearson still regrets the outcome, which, as with the Crown Local Offices, halted another pioneering idea: "If we'd ever got it off the ground [in its original form] it would have been a first in timber frame development going up to five storeys."[17]

Pearson reserves real vehemence for the aesthetic changes, however. Reviewing the resulting presentation report, he bridles: "You see it was never this Noddy vein creation here [The boxed conservatory] is the crucial bit, [..] but this is... this is bullshit."[18]

Whether Pearson's more forceful, contemporary version would have suited the location better is, of course, a moot point, though his stated intention here is perhaps surprising. Regardless, Norwich was a sobering occasion where the compromise Pearson accepts as inherent in architecture left a sour taste, although it maintained his interest in contextualism, passive heating and ventilation and adaptability.

In 1997 Pearson was taken by Bill Howard, a services engineer who had worked on the Makurdi scheme, to a meeting with David Wilson of SERFCA. Pearson came away with a feasibility study for a military band practising room, stores, a music library and administration facilities at Leros Territorial Army Centre, Canterbury, in Kent. Though essentially another chance encounter, "almost 14 years to the day since I had returned from Nigeria", it once more launched a new phase of Pearson's architecture thanks in large part to Wilson, whom Pearson describes as "an inspiring client" with a supportive approach.[19]

The need for a new practising venue for the 30 year old Kohima Band had been established previously, its existing space being part of a storage shed which produced a poor quality of sound and was too small, the enforced close proximity of the musicians to each other risking damage to their hearing.[20] The same

Fishergate solution: diagram of the natural climate control planned, with extreme and mid-point conditions illustrated. Norwich Cathedral sightlines are retained even in the inner zone.

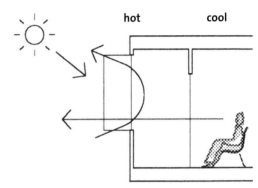

Summer

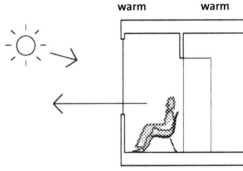

Mid-season

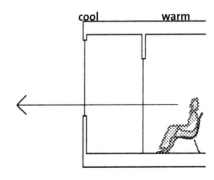

Winter

Right
Leros Territorial Army Centre interior with acoustic sail and sound-absorbing curtains and light box above. Air ducts are in the zone above the stained plywood panels.

Opposite
Early elevations of the practising room exterior with the stepped, drum-like profile caused by planned external air conditioning pipe runs; one depicts timber cladding ideas. And below a section through a brick wall solution.

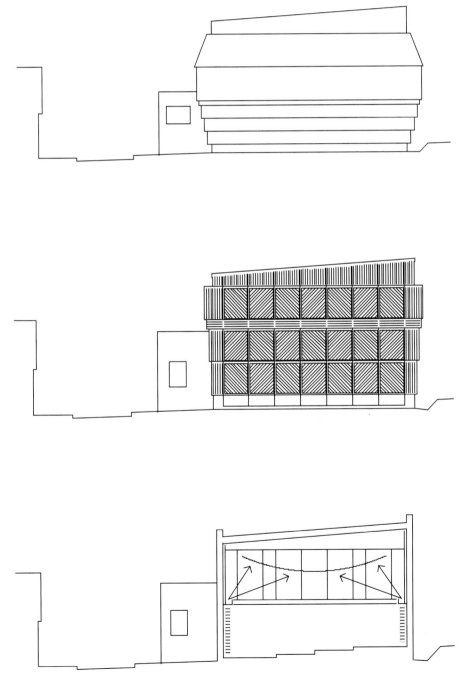

shed also housed the band's equipment and music library in very basic surroundings.

It was determined that building a new, purpose-designed practising room was the most appropriate solution, freeing the existing shed to be remodelled for secure storage of instruments and the music library and better offices.

In taking the job forward, Pearson used the same technique he and David Gray had employed in their international hospital schemes to engage with users. Notes Pearson:

> The architect and the user worked together on interactive briefing and design: testing objectives against design limitations, adjusting the objectives and testing the design again, until a satisfactory compromise was found between the two. Discussions of the users requirements continued to completion of the project to ensure that the user's requirements were being provided.[21]

For the practising room, the critical issue was how to create "the biggest volume we could afford" to allow room for sound to expand into and decay and to create the right overall acoustic.[22] The transfer of sound to the exterior of the building had also to be reduced to minimise disturbance to neighbours (houses stood close to the site boundary) whilst the reverse was also true; noise from outside could not disrupt the music inside.

Utilising the sound absorption qualities of concrete, a structure of solid concrete block walls and pre-cast concrete plank roof was chosen. This was also quick to erect. Windows—expensive, given the specialised requirements of the building—were omitted.

Within, wood studwork covered by plasterboard and stained plywood gave thermal and some acoustic insulation. A continuous fabric curtain around the lower part of the walls provided an additional layer of sound reduction. This was supplemented by an ingenious fabric "acoustic sail" hung from the ceiling with stainless steel yacht rigging, allowing further modification of the sound pattern whilst maintaining the maximum volume of the building structure above it in a way that a conventional suspended ceiling would not.[23] The sail also served to reflect light downward from the simple lighting boxes around the walls.

Environmental control for the new space centred around the specifics of the building's usage: short periods of occupation which generated high levels of humidity, and a need for minimal noise both inside and outside. This was achieved by installing a mechanised system which could respond rapidly to demand and would work in conjunction with the structural insulation. To minimise internal noise, as much equipment as possible was mounted externally, roof-mounted as with many of Pearson's buildings. Attenuators within the system reduced sound transmission in both directions.

For the facades of the practising room, various cladding alternatives were explored by Pearson with the twin aims of affording weather protection for the structural concrete walls and defining the aesthetic character of the building. The latter was especially important given the lack of fenestration.

Timber was initially preferred, drawing on Pearson's earlier designs for Swansea and Leicester, in stained panels whose striated finish ran—in alternative versions—vertically or at angles. During the evolution of the environmental control system, various lagged pipes of around 150 millimetres in diameter were to have run around the exterior perimeter of the building about half way up the walls, creating a 'swelling'. Since the pipes would need to be maintained, Pearson made a virtue of the situation by incorporating access panels and differentiating this area through an alteration in the cladding panel arrangement. To find a link back to the language of Burne House's purposeful cladding, albeit in a very different material, is engaging. That the resulting building profile resembled a drum is entirely coincidental. Pearson's client was uncomfortable with timber, however, having had experience of the maintenance expense associated with it (when untreated). Asking Pearson to investigate the cost of brick and discovering that it was broadly the same, he requested this be used instead. Coupled with changes to the environmental conditioning that first reduced and then eliminated the swelling, this led to the final shape and treatment of the exterior—a straight-walled, brick-clad near double cube. Pearson took

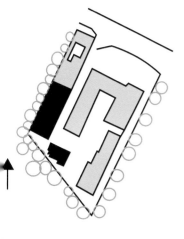

Opposite
exterior of the recruitment centre
building, with its 'slot' windows
and timber cladding.

Top
Interior of the garage; note
the structural members,
distinct from the skin, and
coiled exhaust hoses.

Bottom
Site plan of the Bletchley complex.
Note the stepped plan of the
recruitment centre building.

cues from adjacent buildings on the barracks site and an eighteenth century boundary wall when designing the brick panels:

> The drill hall, across the drive from the stores building, probably built between the wars, set the style with plain red bricks, soldier lintels and soldier string courses. The stores building echoed this style and added brown brick quoins. With a low cost brick for the new building it was not possible to get a very close match in colour and texture but it is in the same range and continues the soldier courses and quoins. The panels of brickwork were very carefully proportioned.[24]

To complete the scheme, the interior of the existing shed was reordered with storage racking under the highest point of the ridged roof to maximise capacity and a mezzanine above that, naturally lit from a rooflight, for the music library.

The practising room at Leros is one of Pearson's most fascinating built projects, a compact, economic and attractive building which has served its users admirably. Despite the very specialised nature of the practising room, many standard components were employed; despite the limited budget, performance was not compromised. Indeed, "On completion the acoustic was checked and pronounced to be of a concert standard."[25] In keeping with Pearson's longstanding philosophy, maintenance costs were also minimised by such measures as the choice of materials and even the placing of the internal light boxes at head height to ease access.

As for the users, Kohima Band members enjoy their new room and have improved the standard of their performance. Their surroundings are healthier, as is their bank balance since they have had more engagements and also hire out the room to others.

Other jobs for SERFCA followed, including alterations to existing structures and new buildings such as a cadets' block with natural lighting and ventilation at Banbury, Oxfordshire, before Pearson's next major project for this client—stores, offices and a garage at Bletchley Territorial Army Centre, Buckinghamshire. The first element of this scheme to be executed was a two-storey building containing offices, a rest room and a recruiting suite. With a partially stepped plan, the block has a shallow mono-pitch roof and is both timber-framed and clad, as intended at Pearson's Leicester arts centre. Sheathed in distinctive vertically-grooved wood, the block also features an irregular arrangement of windows that includes tall, narrow units and short, wide ones, calling to mind Mayford school.

The second element was a "high performance garage" for the storage, maintenance and repair of the vehicles used by the unit based at the centre.[26]

Rather more complex than a standard commercial garage, the new building was constructed on a steel frame. Front and rear walls were formed from equally-spaced I-beam upstands connected across their tops by further I-beams; for the rear wall only (to allow for unobstructed doors at the front), additional strength came from tubular members running from the top of selected I-beams diagonally to the ground. Each side wall was similar but comprised a single I-beam upstand with a tubular member on each side of it.

For the roof, a single long I-beam ran between corresponding pairs of front and rear wall upstands, thus spanning the depth of the entire building and creating an unobstructed interior. These roof I-beams were cross-braced to each other with more tubular members. The garage is clad in corrugated metal sheeting and folding/sliding doors allow the front to be opened along almost all of its width.

Services within the envelope thus created included a heavy-duty power supply for the vehicles to be plugged into and a pipe network which leads to the exterior from flexible, large-bore hoses stored on drums just below the ceiling that are unrolled and connected to the vehicles' exhausts. This allows engines to be run for long periods for testing without fumes filling the garage.

As a pure machine building the Bletchley garage, completed in 2006, might appear an unusual scheme to close this chapter, but it is in fact as powerful an example of Pearson's work as any of his earlier works. In its clear expression, even celebration, of its structure (brightly coloured and distinct from its skin), its use of dry-fit components and its existence as a servant/served space, it is a true inheritor of much of the philosophy demonstrated at the Crown Local Offices and Burne House, providing a deep continuity with these earlier projects. And fittingly, transport buildings, including hangars and garages, are perhaps the final major building type to have emerged in architecture, critics in the early Modernist period recognising them as equally worthy of coverage: "Curiously enough, these sheds, though built of different materials and being in their baldness of outline the very antithesis of a cathedral, are yet built upon the same structural principles."[27] The SERFCA buildings portray Pearson's attention to user need, acute sensitivity to materials and service provision and iterative planning process as vividly as any of the projects considered thus far. This should not be surprising for, as the present work has attempted to show, Pearson has maintained a remarkable consistency throughout his practice, despite the "violent change in direction professionally about every ten years" which he has noticed.[28]

Co-incidentally this change occurred most recently the same year in which Bletchley was finished, when diverse difficulties required relocation back to Lancaster and a reshaping of his practice.

The final chapter examines the result of this latest adaptation, and brings the story of Pearson's architecture up to date.

1   MP, in conversation with the author, 15 February 2008.

2   MP, "Business Centre, Penllergaer, Swansea", 17 August 1993.

3   MP, fax to Dan Phillips, 12 August 1993; MP, note, design sketch sheet, 10 August 1993.

4   MP, "Business Centre, Penllergaer, Swansea".

5   MP, in conversation with the author, 7 August 2008. Joseph Paxton designed calico blinds for the Crystal Palace to act as sun shields.

6   MP, note, design sketch sheet, 7 August 1993. The author has explored this issue with reference to the adaptability of post-war buildings; see Chris Rogers, "Lost World? Post-war buildings in peril", *The Twentieth Century Society Newsletter*, Spring 2006; MP, in conversation with the author, 7 August 2008.

7   MP, Business Centre, Penllergaer, Swansea.

8   MP, note, design sketch sheet, 9 August 1993.

9   Michael Pearson Associates practice brochure, c. 1996.

10   MP, in conversation with the author, 7 August 2008.

11 & 12   MP, nearly 20 years before this commission, writing in *A note on our attitude to design*, 1977, Pearson noted the importance of flexibility in dwelling space intended for elderly people, for whom "it may be important to have several locations for the bed".

13   MP, in conversation with the author, 31 July 2008.

14   MP, in conversation with the author, 7 August 2008.

15   MP, in conversation with the author, 31 July 2008. The Malta reference also reflects a personal fondness for the Mediterranean which Pearson would often sail. A professional foray abroad once more around this time saw Pearson design a sizeable private residence to be inserted into the twelfth century Castillo de Portezuelo, Caceres, Spain, using walls of glass to preserve views toward original stone walls and with sympathetic Moorish-style detail. A central stair identical to that at Lancaster Royal Grammar School was planned. The project, from 1988, was not built.

16   MP, in conversation with the author, 7 August 2008.

17 & 18   MP, in conversation with the author, 31 July 2008.

19   MP, note, 16 September 2008; MP, in conversation with the author, 16 November 2008.

20   The band is named after the successful defence by the Royal West Kent Regiment of the road junction at Kohima against a major Japanese offensive towards India in 1944.

21   MP, "The Kohima Band, 3 Princess of Wales's Royal Regiment: new accommodation, Leros TA centre, Canterbury", 15 July 2008.

22   MP, note, 16 September 2008.

23 & 24   MP, "The Kohima Band, 3 Princess of Wales's Royal Regiment: new accommodation, Leros TA centre, Canterbury".

25 & 26   MP, note, 16 September 2008.

27   Quoted from an early edition of *The Architects' Journal* in *The Twenties*, *The Architects' Journal* centenary issue, Emap Business Communications, 1995.

28   MP, letter to the author, 2 November 2006.

9 | Pearson Today

You see things that you don't see on photographs. You just have to go. Just have to go, check everything, check everybody; I'm having a land survey done with the levels which will mean something by the time I get it.[1]

At the age of 77 Pearson continues to practise, hurtling around the country by rail with Paxton-like industry, often for the site inspection which he considers a critical preliminary step in a design.[2] Allowing him to learn the "nuance of every slope and every change in level from those slopes to other slopes", its value is evident in the reply to the land seen in his architecture.[3]

Like his father and grandfather Pearson continues to enter competitions, such as that to remodel Morecambe's seafront arising from the recent revitalisation of the Midland Hotel, and propose improvements to his home town, where he is "trying to persuade them to build a new parish hall next to the 1870s church, so that should be fun in terms of listed building consent."[4]

Driving around Lancaster, Pearson — passionate about good design in all its forms — offers informed, eloquent, concise but withering criticism of much of the built environment, from road sightlines and traffic signs to the architecture of the university's new halls of residence, and from the lack of an appropriate municipal gateway to the city to the poor layout of the new covered market's stalls. As ever, the edges of buildings particularly exercise him:

In Barcelona and Gerona the local authority dealt with the common land, the pavements, the squares, and had those designed by — well, certainly in Barcelona they started working with students at the school of architecture to deal with urban design, and left the buildings to the architects. I think that's very important, and it's not happening in a place like Lancaster, for instance; the space between buildings is diabolical.[5]

Further afield, Pearson shows deep knowledge of the area's topography — its fells, dry stone walls, climate — history, tradition and agriculture, and theorises on the symbiosis of railway service frequency and village life.

Pearson's return to Lancaster, full circle, therefore seems appropriate, even if unplanned.

Though unlooked for, these changes in circumstance have always stimulated Pearson to produce his freshest and most progressive work, even if not all of it was realised. Of an innovative housing development he designed for an enterprising local builder, only the roads serving the street where he now lives with his third wife were rendered concrete, whilst in other cases

A lot of people finished my designs! When I did the masterplan and marina at Agia Napa in the southeast corner of Cyprus, [a] site for about four hotels and holiday villas and then there's a yacht haven [...;] flying back from Damascus I used to see this blasted thing being built, with the roads in the same shape, almost, as my drawings for which I never got a penny![6]

Despite these fluctuations, Pearson has no plans to retire. Efficiency and speed of reaction are as important now as when he worked abroad in the 1970s or in London in the 1990s, and Pearson still follows his highly effective tenet of working in small skilled teams, now with friend and colleague Gordon Strain.

The process remains as important as any amount of theory, but as has been shown, the word should not be read as limiting the creation of Pearson's architecture; rather, it is an enabler. A frequent letter writer on for example housing and traffic planning, Pearson also unsurprisingly decries a lack of end user consultation in current hospital procurement policy, concluding that "The public purse appears unwilling to pay for 'planning to minimise future regret': it will surely pay later."[7]

When I started to practise architecture, we were already aware of the short life of building solutions and the world of the built environment was experiencing an increasing rate of change.

Whilst teaching architecture in the UK and the USA, we knew that economics and information technology would significantly change the way in which buildings would be used during their life span. This led me to innovative designs of local offices for central government and ultimately to the design of the London telecommunications centre which had to house new generations of equipment which were unknown before construction started. I came to this project because of my considerable experience of the complex building services required for hospitals: one providing a working environment for the treatment and diagnosis of people and the other for equipment providing a service which everyone uses. The problems of change were comparable. This experience of designing for information technology now has applications in most building types.

The rate of change is accelerating and we no longer know what working patterns will emerge but we suspect that fewer people will do more and more. One thing about which I feel is certain is our assessment of the essential needs for face-to-face contact, from which springs a variety of opportunities.

I believe we are moving towards cheaper and quicker construction, less reliant on expensive energy costs and easier to maintain, as my recent building experience has shown. In particular, my experience overseas of extreme alternatives of building technology, climatic conditions, skilled manpower, social expectations, economic restraints and cultural mores. This has heightened my awareness in designing buildings.

The conclusion of our striving for excellence must be to offer visual delight and reflect the image of our current and very special local culture.

Michael Pearson

London, 1994
In the depths of the recession when most construction stopped.

The deaths of Reyner Banham, Jim Stirling, Roy Landau, Cedric Price and others inevitably focus attention on those remaining, especially if still in practice.[8] An exhibition, Portrait of a Practice — Pearson Centenary, was held at the AA in 2004 and brought the firm's work to new audiences, student and professional alike; the present work will, it is hoped, extend that. Pearson himself is now keen to develop a web presence, noting, deadpan, that in 20 years' time he will not be able to rely on personal contacts and happenstance to obtain work; the prescient Olaf Helmer would be pleased.

Pearson has always taken a non-dogmatic view of his role, at odds, perhaps, with the still popularly promoted image of the architect. Recognising that "Unfortunately, architects' experiments are life size", Pearson has stated that: "No decisions can be totally right. One can only hope that they are less wrong than they might be and that they stay that way with the passage of time."[9]

He remains of this view today, as he enjoys a happy family life. And asked if he is happy professionally, he is characteristically unsentimental: "I don't know about happiness, but I'm content!".[10]

1   MP, in conversation with the author, 12 February 2008.
2   Joseph Paxton's extraordinarily complex and exhausting daily (and often nightly) business travels on the then-new rail system are glimpsed in John McKean's superb *Crystal Palace*, 1994. Pearson shows similar energy and mastery of the rail network and its timetables.
3   MP, in conversation with the author, 7 August 2008.
4   Restored and remodelled by Urban Splash, the hotel reopened in June 2008. The Morecambe central promenade development, aimed at rejuvenating the surrounding area, continues, somewhat controversially, at the time of writing. Pearson submitted his own ideas for the development; MP, in conversation with the author, 7 August 2008.
5   MP, in conversation with the author, 29 February 2008.
6   MP, in conversation with the author, 22 July 2008.
7   MP, letter to *The Architects' Journal*, 22 April 2003.
8   In 1988, 1992, 2001 and 2003 respectively.
9   MP, quoted in "The Architect V The Housewife", *Ideal Home*, c. 1970; MP, "Week by Week", *Building Design*, 13 April 1979.
10 MP, in conversation with the author, 7 August 2008.

1933 Charles Michael Pearson born 6 March in Morecambe, Lancaster

1941 Starts Lancaster Royal Grammar School, preparatory instruction before starting main school in 1943

1951 First year undergraduate, Manchester University

1957 Graduates Batchelor of Arts with Honours in Architecture
Assistant architect, Richard Sheppard and Partners

1958 Opens London office of Charles B Pearson & Son for his father

1959 Elected Associate of the Royal Institute of British Architects

1960 Concrete block research tour of the United States promoted by Cement and Concrete Association and organised by Portland Cement Association
Visited Philip Johnson and Louis Khan, and several of their buildings

1961 Partner, Charles B Pearson Son & Partners (to 1977)

1962 Unit master, Architectural Association School of Architecture, London (to 1966)

1963 Elected Fellow of the Royal Society for the Encouragement of Arts, Manufactures & Commerce

1966 Design Critic, Bartlett, University of London (to 1967)

1967 Visiting professor, School of Architecture and Allied Arts, Department of Architecture, University of Oregon, United States
Visiting design critic, Berkeley, Stanford, UCLA, Illinois at Chicago Circle, Philadelphia, Carnegie Tech, Columbia, United States
Visited Kaiser hospitals, California, United States
Visited NASA complexes at Cape Kennedy and Houston, United States

1970 Elected Fellow of the Royal Institute of British Architects

1971 Council member, Architectural Association
Honorary Librarian, Architectural Association (to 1972)

1972 Honorary Treasurer, Architectural Association (to 1973)

1973 President, Architectural Association (to 1974)

1977 Senior Partner, with Charles E Pearson, Pearson International and Pearson Associates (to 1982)

1979 Senior Partner with Frank O Chidi, Pearson Chidi Associates, Lagos (to 1983)

1982 Principal, Michael Pearson Associates

2003 Partnership with Abigail Pearson (to 2005)

2006 Principal, Pearson Architects

PEARSON PRACTICE — SUCCESSES IN ARCHITECTURAL COMPETITIONS

Date	Project	Prize
1905	Preston Secondary School	Third Prize
1914	Concrete Cottage	Second Prize
1920	Southport Secondary School	Second Prize
1921	Glasgow High School	Selected
1922	Labour Saving Bungalow	Daily Mail Book
1931	Ramsay Grammar School	First Prize
1932	Southampton Grammar School	Second Prize
1932	Birmingham Mansion House	Highly Commended
1936	Llandudno Hospital	First Prize
1936	Harpenden Public Hall	Third Prize
1936	Newport Civic Centre	Third Prize
1937	Scunthorpe Civic Centre	First Prize
1938	Chester Royal Infirmary	Second Prize
1960	Medical Centre for Wales	Second Prize
1961	Boston Hospital	Highly Commended
1967	Ashton-in-Makerfield Crown Local Office	First Prize

DRAWINGS EXHIBITED AT THE ROYAL ACADEMY

1906	County Sessions House, Preston, for the Lancashire County Architect
1920	Memorial Hall and Cross, Glasson Dock, Lancaster
1921	Secondary School Competition, Southport
1921	New Kinema, Carnforth, Lancaster
1921	Domestic work. House and Cottages, Lancaster
1924	Lowood, house, Arnside, Westmoreland
1925	Domestic Work. Houses at Bare, Arkholme and Arnside
1925	Warehouse and Offices, Cable Street, Lancaster
	Manserghs, Cable Street; demolition for Sainsbury's supermarket
1925	Detail of a portion of a Public Building
1926	Houses at Carus Park, Lancaster
1929	Store for Reddrop & Co, Cheapside and Lower Church Street, Lancaster
1930	Village Hall, Arnside, Westmoreland
1931	Ramsay Grammar School, Isle of Man, Competition
1931	Moorgarth, house, Lancaster
1932	Mansion House Competition, Birmingham
1938	Civic Centre Competition, Scunthorpe

This represents the fullest log of projects in which Michael Pearson has been involved that it has been possible to collate. Built and unbuilt works, including competition entries, are listed, chronologically by start date. All works were built unless indicated. Individual architects within the practice who also worked on a given job are not shown, although where Pearson worked with another firm or external practitioner this is recorded. Interiors not involving structural alteration or architectural intervention are not included.

There is no formal archive relating to the work of the Pearson family practice, principally as a result of its split in 1977 and the subsequent fate of its offshoots. Since 1904 it has been titled and constituted as follows:

1904	Charles B Pearson (sole practitioner)
1931	Charles B Pearson & Son (Charles B Pearson, Charles E Pearson)
1945	Charles B Pearson & Son (Charles E Pearson)
1961	Charles B Pearson Son & Partners (Charles E Pearson, senior partner, with George Lovell, Peter Lund Michael Pearson as partners) Edward Mason was made a partner later
1977	Pearson Associates (for works in Britain), Pearson International (for works abroad) (Michael Pearson, with Charles E Pearson assisting in various roles) Other former partners continued to practise from the old Lancaster and Manchester offices until 1990
1982	Michael Pearson Associates (etc.; a number of name changes to present) (Michael Pearson, with (for periods) daughter Abigail Pearson as partner, daughter Karine as administrator, various associates and consultants)
2006	Pearson Architects (Michael Pearson as sole practitioner)

Pearson recounts how Charles E's position shifted following the 1961 reshaping, perhaps inevitably:

I think what happened was that father was a great designer, [but] after the war he suddenly became a manager of the practice.[1]

Pearson observed how even job architects came to have a "a lot of control over what they did, what they designed",[2] whilst at partners' meetings he expected criticism of current schemes akin to his AA experience but found "we never talked about architecture!".[3] Later expansion worsened the situation with the burden of administration taking over. Both Pearsons left in 1977 after a difficult period but continued to practice together, maintaining the continuity began by Charles B.

When the Lancaster and Manchester offices finally closed in 1990, no job records were kept; indeed, Pearson recalls being telephoned in London by a colleague, Geoff Leather, and informed that everything was being literally thrown onto a skip and that he should return right away if

he wished to save anything. He did so and this, plus other papers retained during his career, comprise the primary documentary sources consulted for the present work.

Brochures, texts and presentation files constitute the bulk of the material, along with contemporary photographic negatives of many built projects from northern and southern offices of the firm. Other negatives found their way to the archives of various institutions, whilst others have been destroyed or lost. In some cases the inheritors of historic images simply could not be located.

Fortunately considerable material survives on Burne House, including many working drawings and a very large quantity of original correspondence covering the entire project, arranged by party, only a small percentage of which could be reviewed in the time available. This comprises the complete on site record of the clerk of the works

Preserved partnership meeting minutes from 1961 to1969 proved vital in establishing timelines.

Supplementing the above for the present work has been several hours of recorded interviews and conversations with Pearson conducted by the author in London, Lancaster and elsewhere.

As to the future; Pearson would like his material to have a secure home with an appropriate body (a complete run of *244* has been lodged with the AA, but this is the only institutional holding at present) and has suggested Lancaster University to maintain the local connection; it may be that publication of the present work will act as a catalyst for that, enabling later generations to reflect on the Pearson legacy in full.

1-3 MP in conversation with the author, 29 February 2008.

1957–1958	**Weeks Hall**	Imperial College London, South Kensington, London. Employed at Richard Sheppard & Partners
1957–1958	**Defects investigations**	Technical College, Burton-on-Trent, Staffordshire. Employed at Richard Sheppard & Partners
	Petrol filling stations	National Benzole ltd: Gidea Park, Romford; Abbey Road, London, SE1; Swaddlingcote, Derbyshire; Bootle, Liverpool.
1959–1960	**Almshouses**	Lindow Square, Lancaster, Lancashire
1956–1966	**Dining Room**	Lancaster Royal Grammar School , Lancaster, Lancashire
1960–1963	**Parish Hall**	Middleton, Morecambe, Lancashire
1960–1965	**Shackcliffe Green School**	Moston, Manchester, Greater Manchester
1963	**Spastics Training Centre**	Lancaster, Lancashire Landscaping scheme only; Centre built but scheme not executed
1965–1966	**Approved School**	Mayford, Woking, Surrey Demolished
1965–1966	**Crown Local Office**	Lancaster, Lancashire Commission (unbuilt)
1969	**School and District swimming pool**	Turton, Bolton, Lancashire
1969–1972	**Ewen Studio**	Biddestone, Wiltshire
1967	**Crown Local Office**	Ashton-in-Makerfield, Greater Manchester Competition entry: first prize (unbuilt)
1969–1977	**Burne House Telecommunications Centre**	Paddington, London
1970-onwards		Residential restorations, refurbishments, conversions, extensions. Various sites in Britain. Includes period, listed and public sector properties
1971	**Pompidou Centre**	Paris, France Competition entry (unbuilt)
1971	**Health centres**	Nigeria Unbuilt
1971	**Sports halls**	Nigeria Unbuilt
1972	**Housing**	Wattsville, Newport, Wales Unbuilt
1974	**Housing and road layout**	Burrow Beck, Lancaster, Lancashire Priced kit of parts for extension and alteration. Road layout only executed
1974	**Commercial Centre**	Manama, Bahrain Residences convertible to offices over a souk. Design scheme (unbuilt)
1974–1979	**University Teaching Hospital**	Damascus, Syria Design, construction documents, tenders, equipment and finance (unbuilt)
1973–1975	**Tourist Village**	Agia Napa, Cyprus Development plan (unbuilt)
1976	**Hotels and holiday villas,**	Evvia, Greece (unbuilt)
1976	**General Hospital**	Ahwaz, Iran For National Iranian Oil Company (unbuilt)
1976	**National Assembly Buildings**	Abu Dhabi, United Arab Emirates Competition entry (unbuilt)
1976	**Tourist complexes**	Northern Regions, Iraq Design study with Cementation International (unbuilt)
1976	**Paediatric Hospital**	Basra, Iraq Feasibility study (unbuilt)
1976	**Orthopaedic Hospital**	Baghdad, Iraq Design study (unbuilt)
1977	**Community Hospitals**	Venezuela Design schemes with Shanning International (unbuilt)

1977	**Community Hospitals**	Bolivia Design schemes with Shanning International (unbuilt)
1977	**Health Centres**	Ecuador Design schemes for Ministry of Health (unbuilt)
1977	**Landhaus and administration buildings**	Vienna, Austria Competition entry (unbuilt)
1977–1979	**University Teaching Hospital**	Ilorin, Kwara State, Nigeria Design and construction documents (unbuilt)
1979	**Commercial Centre**	Amman, Jordan Offices and restaurant over shopping complex and parking, design scheme, tender and finance with Tarmac International (unbuilt)
1979	**Corniche Maternity Hospital extension**	Abu Dhabi, United Arab Emirates Design scheme with Joannou & Paraskevaides
1980	**Awolowo University, Ado Ekiti**	Akure State, Nigeria (unbuilt) Strategic planning alternatives (unbuilt)
1980–1983	**Federal University of Technology**	Makurdi, Benue State, Nigeria Four colleges, all residences: development plan and strategic infra-structure; 17 temporary buildings completed, with Frank O Chidi
1980	**Seth PD Hinduja Hospital**	Bombay, India Medical and mechanical services planning: architecture by IM Kadri
1981	**Alexandria International Hospital**	Alexandria, Egypt Hospital at university for private patients of medical school consultants: design scheme for American Medical International (unbuilt)
1981	**Special Amenity Hospital**	Port Harcourt, Rivers State, Nigeria Design scheme with Frank O Chidi (unbuilt)
1981	**Motel**	Port Harcourt, Rivers State, Nigeria Design scheme with Frank O Chidi (unbuilt)
1981	**Paediatric Hospital**	Port Harcourt, Rivers State, Nigeria Design scheme with Frank O Chidi (unbuilt)
1981	**Orthopaedic Hospital**	Port Harcourt, Rivers State, Nigeria Design scheme with Frank O Chidi (unbuilt)
1982	**Tête Défense**	Paris, France Competition entry with Les Pustelnik (unbuilt)
1984–1997	**British Telecom projects**	Various London sites within M25 ring road including, Acton, Chelsea, Chingford, Croydon, Eltham, Hainhault, Hampton, Heathrow, Kingston, London Monument, Merton, Putney, Stapleford, Streatham, Surbiton, Vauxhall, Walthamstow, Wandsworth, Wanstead, West Drayton, Wimbledon, Woodford Alterations for new apparatus, building surveys, office designs, interiors, car parking, landscaping
1985	**Marble Arch remodelling**	Hyde Park, London Competition entry (unbuilt)
1986	**Tourism Complex**	Vieux Fort, St Lucia For the Minister of Tourism (unbuilt)
1987	**St Peter's Church**	Ipswich, Suffolk Conversion to managed workspace, design scheme for Stansall (Properties) ltd (unbuilt)
1988	**Castillo de Portezuelo**	Cáceres, Spain Design scheme: luxury house within 12c walls built by Moors (unbuilt)
1989	**Trilion Television Studio**	Trocadero Centre, Leicester Square, London Design and administration with Patrick Garnett, design and construction in 14 weeks
1992	**All Saints Church**	Bradford, West Yorkshire Ideas competition entry (unbuilt)

1993	**Richard Attenborough Centre for Disability and the Arts**	University of Leicester, Leicester, Leicestershire Competition entry (unbuilt)
1993	**Business Centre**	Swansea, Wales Competition entry (unbuilt)
1995	**Residential and retail development**	Fishergate, Norwich, Norfolk Design scheme for Stansall (Properties) ltd (unbuilt)
1995	**Bus station**	Walsall, West Midlands Competition entry (unbuilt)
1997–2000	**Territorial Army Centre**	Canterbury, Kent Band practising room, music library, stores, administration, Uxbridge, London
1998	**Uxbridge Magistrates' Court**	Entrance security alterations
1997–2001	**Housing**	London Borough of Hackney, London Defects liability studies
2003–2006	**CIPFA**	1–3 Robert Street, London, WC2 Terrace designed by Adam brothers, listed grade II*; upgrading office facilities
2003–2006	**Housing on the Holborn Estate**	London Borough of Camden, London Repairs, including 25 listed buildings
2006	**Morecambe Central Promenade Development**	Morecambe, Lancashire Competition entry for flats, conference centre and landscaping (unbuilt)
1998–present	**Projects for the South East Reserve Forces' and Cadets' Association:**	Various locations including, Ascot, Ashford, Banbury, Beaconsfield, Bletchley, Brize Norton, Buckingham, Chalfont St Peter, Chatham, Faversham, Gravesend, Hailsham, Horsham, Margate, Milton Keynes, Oxford, St Leonards-on-Sea, Wolverton

MP LIST OF CONSULTANTS

Structural Engineers
WG Curtin & Partners
Felix J Samuely & Partners
WS Atkins & Partners
Morgan Omonitan & Partners
Ove Arup & Partners
Buro Happold
Ian Drummond

Building Services Engineers
RW Gregory & Partners
Bertram Done & Partners
Associated Architects & Engineers
Buro Happold
Donald Smith Seymour & Rooley
Ove Arup & Partners
Pentangle
McCarthy Bainbridge

Quantity Surveyors
Holden & Lee
Rider Hunt & Partners
Roland Lay & Partners
DS Leslie & Partners
DAR Roland & Partners
Tillyard
Barry Maltz Associates

Medical Planner
Dr David Kempson Gray

Syrian Culture
Maawia Mardambey
Damascus

Agronomists
James W MacGregor
William JJ Crowe

Lawyer
Pedro Celaya y Salcedo
Pamplona

The following worked with the practice since the end of World War Two. The list is in broadly chronological order. Apologies are extended to anyone who has been inadvertently omitted—this will happily be corrected in any future edition.

London

Charles E Pearson
Michael Pearson
William Cowburn
Cedric Price
Victor Fong
Raymond Hurst
John Stenglehofen
Anthony Dugdale
Yusuf Ismail
Subhi Al-Azzawi
Andrzej Blonski
Peter Colomb
Ruslan Khalid
Shahana Khan
Royston Landau
Sidney Watts
Mary Muecke
Victoria Slaughter
Dennis Sykes
Clive White
Josie Waldie
Stevie Robinson
Han Shi
Andre Blond
Jamie Clarke
Navin Shah
Len Tempest
Geoff Warn
Adi Patell
Sarojini Jaywardene
Roland Paoletti
Leszek Pustelnik
Christine Hawley
Peter Lindsay
Karine Pearson
Stephan Schlau
Micha Bandini
Keith Lipscomb
David Price
Farid Ghali
Gordon Strain
Abigail Pearson

Lancaster to 1977

Charles E Pearson
Peter Pearson Lund
Edward Mason
Walter Berry
Gordon Briggs
Dennis Burneside
Neil Evans
Donald Heptonstall
Geoff Leather
Eva Moorefield
Ken Ormandy
Ian Dickinson
David Jackson
Norman Howarth
Raymond Price
Les Wood
John Stephenson
Jack Waterhouse

Manchester to 1977

George Lovell
Jack Cheetham
David Dickenson
Arnold Moss
David Roberts
Michael Sharp

CREDITS

Cover and Frontispiece	Misha Anikst	p. 100	Burne House, London NW Henk Snoek / RIBA library photographs collection
p. 21	Llandudno Hospital Courtesy of National Museums Liverpool (Stewart Bale collection, Merseyside Maritime Museum)	pp. 108, 109, 111	Burne House, London NW EJ Studios
p. 28	*Architectural Design*	p. 112	Burne House, London NW Misha Anikst
p. 29	*AR Preview*, cover *The Architectural Review*	p. 115	Burne House, London NW Richard Einzig / arcaid.co.uk
p. 36	Scunthorpe Civic Centre Warren Jepson	pp. 118-120	Burne House, London NW Misha Anikst
p. 40	West Cumberland Hospital John Laing Charitable Trust (as holder of the John Laing plc Archive Material)	p. 170	Band Room, Canterbury Charlotte Wood

All other images Michael Pearson

p. 42	Barnsley Hospital John Mills, Mills Media Group
p. 44	Sharoe Green Hospital, Preston Henk Snoek / RIBA library photographs collection
p. 46	Cumberland Infirmary, Carlisle John Mills, Mills Media Group
p. 47	Kilton Hospital, Workshop Peter Lund
p. 48	Ripley School, Lancaster David McKee
p. 50	Carlisle Civic Centre Henk Snoek / RIBA library photographs collection
pp. 54-55	Lancaster Royal Grammar School Hugh de Burgh Galway / *The Architectural Review*
p. 61	Mayford School, Woking Sydney W Newbury / *Building*
pp. 64-66	Turton School Pool, Bolton John Mills, Mills Media Group
pp. , 70, 72, 73	Ewen Studio, Biddestone Richard Einzig / arcaid.co.uk
p. 89	Burne House, London NW Henk Snoek / RIBA library photographs collection
p. 93	Burne House, London NW Richard Einzig / arcaid.co.uk

Dedicated to my parents, for their patience.

I have, of course, to thank Michael first of all, without whom this work would literally not have been possible, as well as Misha, for his excellent design, and Duncan, for his composed editing.

Very many thanks are also due to Doreen, Michael's wife, for her hospitality (and superb cooking) during my stays in Lancaster.

I'd also like to thank the following for their help with this book. In no particular order:

Abigail Morris (née Pearson) for a copy of her dissertation on Charles B and Charles E, an invaluable portrait of the first generations of Pearson architects, from which much of chapter 2 derives; John Bowker, alumni assistant at Lancaster Royal Grammar School, for showing Michael and me around on a brisk February term day; Frank Atherley, Christine Garry and Nina Gardiner at North Manchester High School for Girls for so enthusiastically helping me trace the recent history of Shackcliffe Green; George Brinkhurst and Nick Hickman at Surrey County Council for similar assistance with Mayford school; Richard and Andi Ewen for a wonderful visit to Willowbrook (including an excellent lunch), and Andi for additional written material on the studio addition; Alyson Rogers at the National Monument Record Enquiries and Research Services for speedily-supplied listing information; Simon Bradley, Kenneth Powell and Alan Powers for valuable initial advice, and Simon for always being uncomplainingly available for nuggets of information and Alan for assistance with the AA independence issue; Howard Tustin and particularly Chris Jackson of Serco for information on Turton pool, and Joanne Shaw at Turton High School Media Arts College for contact information; Stuart Mead and Paul Brumwell at the BRE for handling my historical test data enquiries; Jenny Griffiths at Mills Media for locating historical negatives of Turton; Colin Williams at Yorkshire Photographic Union, Caroline Spillane at Warrens and Mike Hargreaves of New Dimension Photography for the ultimately sad story of the Scunthorpe negatives; Eleanor Winyard at Northamptonshire Record Office (Archive) for finding the Carlisle Civic Centre negatives; Karen Bradshaw at Taylor Woodrow for trying to find Burne House construction negatives; Jonathan Makepeace at the RIBA Library Photographs Collection for Hank Snoek negatives; Navin Shah for reminiscences on his involvement with Burne House; Elain Harwood for identifying the crucial West Midlands Gas Board offices and supplying an important reference for same; Ian Liddell for help with Vienna and Abu Dhabi; Gary MacLeod, my indefatigable personal IT helpdesk; and last but by no measure least, Catherine and Julie for inspiration and support throughout.

That old convention applies, though: all of the above contributed, but any errors are mine alone.

Chris Rogers

Richard Ewen

During the closing stages of the preparation of this book for printing, I was shocked and saddened to learn of the death of Richard Ewen in April 2009. Richard had been suffering from ill-health for some time, but, as mentioned in chapter 5, had been recovering.

I am extremely glad that I was able to meet Richard at his home to discuss and share his experience of the wonderful studio that Michael Pearson designed for him, and hope that some of the relationship between the two – artist and architect, artist and studio – comes across in the text.

In writing this book I have tried to include as many quotations as possible subject to word count, and I am particularly pleased now to have managed to include the most significant portions of the fascinating conversations that occurred between Richard, Michael and myself. Perhaps I might end this note by including one that almost got away, as a final tribute to the gentle and welcoming man I met that day; as we mentioned the budget for the studio project, Richard quipped "We artists don't have things like that!"

COLOPHON

©2010 Black Dog Publishing Limited, London, UK,
the author and architect. All rights reserved.

Chris Rogers has asserted his moral right as the author
of the text *The Power of Process: The Architecture of
Michael Pearson*.

Design by Anikst Design, London.

Black Dog Publishing Limited
10a Acton Street
London WC1X 9NG
United Kingdom

Tel: +44 (0)20 7713 5097
Fax: +44 (0)20 7713 8682
info@blackdogonline.com
www.blackdogonline.com

British Library Cataloguing-in-Publication Data. A CIP
record for this book is available from the British Library.

ISBN 978 1 906155 73 5

Black Dog Publishing Limited, London, UK, is an
environmentally responsible company. *The Power of
Process: The Architecture of Michael Pearson* is printed
on an FSC certified paper by Melita Press, Malta.

architecture art design
fashion history photography
theory and things

www.blackdogonline.com